TURNING YOUR DREAMS INTO REALITIES

By Glenn Arekion

GLENN AREKION
MINISTRIES publication

Copyright © 2015 Glenn Arekion

All rights reserved under the international copyright law. No part of this book may be reproduced or transmitted in any form or by any means, electronic or mechanical, including photocopying, recording, or by any information storage and retrieval system, without the express, written permission of the author or the publisher. The exception is reviewers, who may quote brief passages in a review.

A Glenn Arekion Ministries Publication
Louisville, KY
glennarekion.org

Published in partnership with
Christian Living Books, Inc.
Largo, MD
christianlivingbooks.com

ISBN 978-1-56229-966-8

Unless otherwise marked, all Scripture quotations are taken from the King James Version of the Bible.

Scripture quotations marked (TLB) are taken from The Living Bible copyright © 1971. Used by permission of Tyndale House Publishers, Inc., Carol Stream, Illinois 60188. All rights reserved. Scripture quotations marked (NASB) are taken from the New American Standard Bible®, Copyright © 1960, 1962, 1963, 1968, 1971, 1972, 1973,1975, 1977, 1995 by The Lockman Foundation. Used by permission of www.Lockman.org. Scripture quotations marked (AMP) are taken from the Amplified® Bible, Copyright© 1954, 1958, 1962, 1964, 1965, 1987 by The Lockman Foundation. Used by permission of Lockman.org. Scripture quotations marked (NKJV) are taken from the New King James Version. Copyright © 1982 by Thomas Nelson, Inc. Used by permission. All rights reserved. Scripture quotations marked (The Message) from THE MESSAGE. Copyright © by Eugene H. Peterson 1993, 1994, 1995, 1996, 2000, 2001, 2002. Used by permission of Tyndale House Publishers, Inc. Scripture quotations marked (ERV) are taken from the Holy Bible: Easy-to-Read Version © 2001 by World Bible Translation Center, Inc. and used by permission. Scripture quotations marked (HCSB) are taken from the Holman Christian Standard Bible®, Copyright © 1999, 2000, 2002, 2003, 2009 by Holman Bible Publishers. Used by permission. Scripture quotations marked (ISV) are taken from the Holy Bible: International Standard Version®. Copyright © 1996-forever by The ISV Foundation. All rights reserved internationally. Used by permission. Scripture quotations marked (NLT) are taken from the Holy Bible, New Living Translation, copyright © 1996, 2004, 2007 by Tyndale House Foundation. Used by permission of Tyndale House Publishers, Inc., Carol Stream, Illinois 60188. All rights reserved. Scripture quotations marked (NET) are from the NET Bible® copyright ©1996-2006 by Biblical Studies Press, L.L.C. Netbible.com. All rights reserved. Used by permission. Scripture quotations marked (BBE) are taken from the 1949/1964 Bible In Basic English which is in the Public Domain. Scripture quotations marked (ARAM) are taken from The Original Aramaic New Testament in Plain English. Translated by Rev. Glenn David Bauscher. Copyright © 2012 Glenn David Bauscher. Used by permission. Scripture quotations marked (GW) is taken from GOD"S WORD® © 1995 God's Word to the Nations. Used by permission of Baker Publishing Group. Scripture quotations marked (NCV) are taken from the New Century Version®. Copyright © 2005 by Thomas Nelson. Used by permission. All rights reserved. Scripture quotations marked (YLT) are taken from The Young's Literal Translation Bible and are in the Public Domain.

Printed in the United States of America

CONTENTS

PART I   **Behold the Dreamer**
Chapter 1: Building the Enterprise   3
Chapter 2: Day Dreamer or Night Dreamer   7
Chapter 3: Imagination 11
Chapter 4: Seven Invalid Excuses. 15

PART II   **Keys To Fulfilling Your Dreams**
Chapter 5: The Virtues and Values of Goal Setting 29
Chapter 6: Why People Do Not Set Goals. 39
Chapter 7: Diversities, Types and Classifications of Goals . . . 49
Chapter 8: Plan of Action and Time Management 59

PART III   **The Satisfaction to Say, "Sweet"**
Chapter 9: Developing Million Dollar Habits 79
Chapter 10: Wisdom Nuggets from Agur's
                Four Little Creatures 91

About the Author 105

PART I

BEHOLD THE DREAMER

BUILDING THE ENTERPRISE

Chapter 1

I want to talk to you about your life, your future and your destiny. As you peruse the pages of this book, there is one thing that is certain: time is passing you by. You are a creature subject to time. The sooner you realize that, the quicker you will be serious about your life, future and destiny. Much has been said, in the last twenty five years, about the importance of dreams and visions. More has been said in regards to a fulfilled life. Yet, there are more dissatisfied people today. It is one thing to have a dream but how do you turn your dream into a living reality? In the next several chapters, I want to show you how to pull something from the invisible to the visible. Many centuries ago, King Solomon said it well:

> The road to promotion is paved with the bricks of obedience.

Through wisdom is an house built and by understanding it is established.
(Proverbs 24:3)

You will need wisdom to build the life of your dreams. You will need wisdom to build your enterprise. That's why Solomon said:

Wisdom is the principal thing, therefore get wisdom. (Proverbs 4:7)

Without wisdom, it becomes difficult to build your life and destiny. Many are struggling to fulfill what they believe they were meant to accomplish in life. They are doing everything and anything they can think of, only to see fruitlessness everywhere. Solomon also gave us insight into this phenomena:

> *If the iron be blunt, and he do not whet the edge, then must he put to more strength: but wisdom is profitable to direct.* (Ecclesiastes 10:10)

Many are wasting energy and money without seeing the desired results. King Solomon reiterates, "wisdom is profitable to direct." What do we mean by wisdom? We mean the divine strategies, which when executed, will give the desired results. Let that sink into your mind and spirit. Wisdom is divine strategies or a divine plan of action. I really like another translation of this verse:

> *Any enterprise is built by wise planning, becomes strong through common sense, and profits wonderfully by keeping abreast of the facts.*
> (Proverbs 24:3 TLB)

From this verse, we can deduct three things about an enterprise:
1. Start up stage – Pioneering and Planning
2. Strengthening stage – Proactivity
3. Security stage – Profits and proceeds

When we hear the word "enterprise" many think of a big business or a big ministry. However, a big business started with a person. The same is true of a big ministry. It started with one person. So, do not limit the word "enterprise" to being just a business. From now on, I want you to see yourself as an enterprise – and, to see your dream as an enterprise.

Don't be deluded into thinking that just because you start something, it will automatically be successful. It is imperative that you go through all three stages.

Many would love to jump from the pioneering stage to the profit stage. Of course, all of us want the profit stage. Notice, however, that between the pioneering stage and the profit stage is the strengthening stage. You cannot avoid the strengthening stage of your enterprise if you want to see the security stage. Starting something is no guarantee of success. Many have started businesses, churches, or

Chapter 1 • Building the Enterprise

ministries only to fail. Why? Although they had a vision, they did not have the strategies and activities to take them to the next level.

The Living Bible says, "Any enterprise... profits wonderfully by keeping abreast of the facts." In this book, I want to give you some facts or instructions to take you from the pioneering stage to the profit stage. Getting you or your enterprise from where it is right now to the next level will require strengthening. The road to promotion is paved with the bricks of obedience to instructions.

Solomon reiterates, "Wisdom hath build her house." (Proverbs 9:1a). The only way you can build your enterprise, your life, your future and destiny is by the divine strategies given to you through wisdom. The Living Bible says, "Any enterprise... becomes strong through common sense..." Here is one thing I have noticed about common sense: common sense is not very common. If it were, everybody would be using it. I am amazed at how many educated and spiritual people can have lofty dreams yet not the common sense to apply some fundamental things to get their dreams off the ground. Some people are so heavenly minded that they are no earthly good.

> Between the pioneering stage and the profit stage is the strengthening stage.

The following pages will provide fundamental instructions. There are some things that you will need to implement, aggressively. There will be things that you will need to cut off. You will have to disconnect emotionally from some things you are tied to. Remember, the road to promotion is paved with the bricks of obedience to instructions.

DAY DREAMER OR NIGHT DREAMER

Chapter 2

For a dream cometh through the multitude of business; and a fool's voice is known by multitude of words. (Ecclesiastes 5:3)

For the dream comes through much effort and the voice of a fool through many words. (Ecclesiastes 5:3 NASB)

You were created to be a winner. Irrespective of where you were born, this crucial fact is unquestionable. You were born a winner – and you were born to win. You could not and would not have been born if you were not a winner. Millions of sperm were swimming towards one egg for fertilization. It was survival of the fittest. The strongest made it in order for conception to take place. When the odds were against you – 200 million to 1 – you overcame and won the race to life in your mother's womb. You began your track record upon the earth as an undisputed winner. Why settle for less now? Whether you realize it or not, there is a sleeping giant inside of you that needs to be awakened. Right now, you may look rough on the outside but there is a diamond on the inside. Your potential will be released and activated through dreams and work.

> You could not and would not have been born if you were not a winner.

We all have dreams and visions. As a child, you dreamed of what you wanted to do with your life. Maybe it has not panned out as you thought. It's never too late. As children, we had great dreams of our future – audacious dreams. We did not anticipate the stumbling blocks because we did not know what they were. Call it innocence or naïveté but as children we dreamed of greatness in our lives. We saw ourselves as superheroes. We saw ourselves "saving the day" like so many cartoon characters we watched on television. We, like those characters, had no sense of fear, weakness or limitations. To our innocent minds, nothing was impossible. It would take others to inform us of what we could not be or do. Unfortunately, some of the "informants" were our own family members, friends and other so-called authority figures.

DEFINING A DREAM

What is a dream? More importantly, what is your dream?
- A dream is something that you want to achieve
- A dream is your cherished aspiration
- A dream is what you would deem as your ideal life
- A dream is the big picture of your preferred life

You want to achieve something great in your life. This is how God wired you. God has given you the ability to dream in order to take you out of a small place into a wealthy place. You are wired to turn defeat into victory and to make something out of what looks like nothing. God has designed you in such a way that there is always a propensity to break out of your borders. God has given you the power of dreams to turn defeat into victory and nothing into something.

TWO TYPES OF DREAMERS

Everybody dreams but not all dreams are effective. Not everybody will fulfill their dreams. There are two types of dreams and dreamers and satan is afraid of only one type.

Chapter 2 • Day Dreamer or Night Dreamer

Night Dreamer

The first type of dream is the one you have at night when you are sleeping, from the recesses of your mind and the multitudes of thoughts. Everyone has dreams like that. When you wake up, you are back to reality. I once dreamed that I was a championship jockey, winning the Derby. When I woke up, I was not on a horse but in my bed. It was real as long as I was asleep. But, the moment I woke up, it was gone. I tried to get it back again when I went to sleep but it was gone.

Day Dreamer

The second type of dreamer is the one who can dream with his eyes wide open. That is the type of dream and dreamer that satan is afraid of. One is a night-dreamer but the other is a day-dreamer and satan is afraid of the day-dreamer. Now, I know day-dreaming is looked upon as time wasting. In reality, day-dreaming is powerful. To be able to visualize yourself successful while in a place of despair is absolutely crucial to success.

> Irrespective of people's opinions, approval or disapproval, keep on dreaming.

I want you to re-awaken the power of dreams today. So many people have stopped dreaming and are just living life one day at a time – never lunging forward in life. When you stop dreaming, your life will be in reverse mode. It is my intent to trigger you into dreaming big again. You *can* have a great life. It does not matter if people accuse you of being a dreamer. This is what the brothers of Joseph said of him:

> *And they said one to another, Behold, this dreamer cometh.* (Genesis 37:19)

Irrespective of people's opinions, approval or disapproval, you need to be like Joseph and keep on dreaming. In this book, I want to give you powerful keys to turn your dreams into reality.

IMAGINATION

Chapter 3

The power to imagine, visualize and dream is crucial to success in life. If the question was asked, "What is the most powerful nation in the world?" Undoubtedly, most would say America. However, many years ago, Ziz Ziglar made a statement that really impacted my life. He said that the most powerful nation is the imagi-nation. As a matter of fact, God also said so. It was in response to man's quest to build the tower of Babel:

> Whatever you can imagine will cause you to soar to greater heights.

> And the LORD said, Behold, the people is one, and they have all one language; and this they begin to do: and now nothing will be restrained from them, which they have imagined to do. (Genesis 11:6)

Imaginations and dreams will shake you from the dust of the ground to the heights of heaven. The people of Babel had high and lofty dreams to defy God. The Almighty did not crush their dream because He does not like dreamers but because they wanted to defy and deny Him. I want you to grasp the fact that God said, "nothing will be restrained from them which they have imagined to do." This is a powerful statement from the mouth of the Almighty! Whatever you can imagine will be the engine that causes you to soar to greater heights. God loves dreamers.

Are you a day-dreamer? I know I am! I do not care where I am right now, what I have or do not have. I have the ability to dream big. It may look like I am in a place of confinement; if I can begin to dream or visualize my miracle and voice it, then it is only a matter of time before it is a living reality in my life.

Many years ago, when I started in ministry, my schedule was not as busy as it is today. First of all, I was twenty one when I went into full time ministry. Many did not give me an opportunity as they thought I was too green behind the ears. In fact, many of my friends and family wanted me to give up on the idea of ministry. They wanted me to get a "proper" job… as they call it. But, I was convinced that I had a calling.

Although my calendar was open, I was very dedicated to my studies and prayer. I would get up early in the morning and accompany my wife to the bus stop as she went to work. Then, I would be in the Word from 9:00 AM till 1:00 PM. From 2:00 PM till 5:00 PM, I would be in prayer. I did this for days, without seemingly any breakthrough.

I would walk around my house, praying in the Spirit, asking God for breakthroughs in ministry. One day, as I was walking around the rooms of my house and praying, I noticed the big map of the world on my wall. I put the map on the floor and began to walk all over it. You see, I knew God had called me to touch the nations of the world with the Gospel. So, I walked on the world map and then rolled myself all over the map. When my wife came home that evening, she posed a question:

"So, Glenn, what have you done today?"

I answered, "Today, I have been all over the world!"

I could see the look of bemusement on her face. She was probably thinking this guy has been spending too much time in the house. This may have looked like a stupid thing to do. Nevertheless, I am reaping the benefits today. Every month, I am on a plane, going to the nations of the world to preach the Gospel of Jesus Christ. I

Chapter 3 • Imagination

imagined it when I had no preaching engagements. When nobody wanted me, I could still imagine great things. It did not cost me a penny to imagine, visualize and dream. Your dreams will bring you to a place where you break out of your borders and limitations. It is not God's will for you to be limited. God Almighty desires to do great things in your life.

> Now unto him that is able to do exceeding abundantly above all we ask or think, according to the power that worketh in us. (Ephesians 3:20)

The phrase "able to do exceeding abundantly" literally means "to transcend all limits and break out of your borders." The Lord wants to break you out of your limitations and into the potential of God. The Word tells us, "God is able" which means He has got the power, ability, might, strength and authority to take you to higher heights. Therefore, you need to remove all limitations. They were mainly imposed by you – or by people around you – but not by God. It is time to remove the excuses that have held you back for so long. Let us look at seven, illegitimate excuses people have used to sabotage their destiny.

> **Transcend all limits and break out of your borders.**

SEVEN INVALID EXCUSES

Chapter 4

Things that people use as limitations and excuses must be eradicated. Although there are many more, I will list seven of the most common excuses people use. Before we proceed, allow me to drop this thought into your mind and spirit: Those who make excuses are only excusing themselves from the greatness that God has for them. You are now entering the no spin zone and the no excuse zone.

> He that is good for making excuses is seldom good for anything else.

He that is good for making excuses is seldom good for anything else.
—Benjamin Franklin

COLOR OF SKIN

I am amazed that in this modern age, people still use their skin color to excuse their lack of results in life. Some deem their skin color as a badge of success and others use skin color as a mark of disgrace. Nothing could be further from the truth. The outer man is made up of dust. It is all dust! Therefore, you have red dust, white dust, black dust, yellow dust and brown dust. At the end of the day, it is still just dust. The word "human" comes from the Latin word *humus* which simply means "dirt" or 'soil". The outer man is dirt. It comes from the soil. Hence, you cannot base success or failure on dirt. It is just a color. Therefore, you are not the wrong color.

You are what you are because God wanted you that way. God does not make mistakes. Your color or pigmentation has got nothing to do with your potential. It is who you are inside, your faith in God, your diligence and your tenacity that determine your success. It is imperative that you do not let the color of your skin be a hindrance in your life. God knew what He was doing when He thought of you. You are unique and you are exactly what God wanted.

While racism does exist in its different tones and forms, no one can stop you if you truly want to succeed. Using your skin color as an excuse for a lack of productivity is more a reflection of poor self-esteem than what is happening externally. Now, when I refer to skin color, I am referring to *all* skin colors. It is not just a black thing. It is also a white thing, yellow, red and brown thing. People of all colors have hang ups about their skin color. It is universal and not just limited to a particular race.

> *I will praise thee; for I am fearfully and wonderfully made; marvelous are thy works; and that my soul knoweth right well.* (Psalm 139:14)

JOHANNESBURG, SOUTH AFRICA

Success is no respecter of skin color. Success has come to people of all colors and races. Why not you? In October 1999, I had the great privilege of hosting Dr. Jerry Savelle for our Island Believer's Convention in Mauritius. I thoroughly enjoyed the convention and his teachings. On the last day, after the final service, I was accompanying him to the airport and asked him a question:

"So, where are you off to next, Brother Jerry?"

His reply, "I am on my way to Johannesburg!"

Again I enquired, "Are you going on vacation there?"

"No, I am going to preach."

Chapter 4 • Seven Invalid Excuses

I questioned him further, "Is it a good church that you will be ministering to?"

His reply, "Yes, it is a great church; it has 14,000 members!"

Now, after he made this statement, my mind went into dreamland. All I could think about was preaching in that church of 14,000 members in Johannesburg. After we said goodbye to Jerry Savelle, my brother was driving me back to meet with another South African friend. All the way back, I could not shake that thought of preaching in a 14,000 member church in Johannesburg. I was quiet on the drive back to the appointment. I allowed my mind to ponder the thought of preaching in a great church.

My brother James asked me, "What's on your mind?"

I replied, "Johannesburg and preaching in that 14,000 member church."

At the appointment, my South African friend met me with a question: "What's on your mind, Glenn?"

I said, "Johannesburg, South Africa."

He enquired further, "What for? Vacation?"

I responded, "No, I want to preach in a church of 14,000 members." I then named the church.

The man replied, "Glenn, forget it! It will never happen!"

I queried, "Well, why not?"

Here was his response, "Well, first of all, you are the wrong color. Secondly, you are too short. Besides, I just can't see how you will get in there."

I responded bluntly, "That's your problem, you cannot see it. But, I see it."

I am glad Jesus did not say, "You shall have what *they* say. He said, you shall have what *you* say." (Mark 11:23) Secondly, I have discovered something about God. He has never made a mistake. Therefore, when God created me and you, He did not make a mistake. You are what you are. The color you are is because God wanted you that way. You are not a mistake. If you are black, be proud of it. If you are white, be proud of it. It does not matter what color you are. What matters is the reality of the new creation.

Guess what? The following year, I was standing in Johannesburg in that church with 14,000 people around me. What the man said I could not do, I DID IT. Allow your mind and imagination to roam today as you read the pages of this book. You will break all kinds of barriers and limitations. Your color is beautiful. Whatever your skin color is, see it as your asset and not a liability. Your nationality is fantastic. Enjoy the person that God created you to be.

If Barack Obama, an African American, can become the president of the United States, then there is no excuse for skin color. If Nelson Mandela can spend twenty seven years in prison and still become the president of South Africa, then, you can do anything. If Tiger Woods can break through and become the world's most famous golfer, then you can dream too. If Andrea Bocelli, the Italian tenor who is blind, can become one of the world's leading opera singers, what's holding you back?

LACK OF EDUCATION

Thank God for formal, academic education. Although it is necessary, it is not the main factor in one's success. While a formal education can provide a platform to push you to greater heights, for millions of so called "academics", it has not done so for them. Many of them are depressed or alcoholics. There are many people with degrees after their names who are failures in their lives.

Chapter 4 • Seven Invalid Excuses

If you feel that you did not grab your chance when you were younger or simply that the opportunity was not there for you, it is not a problem. With the internet at your disposal, you can learn anything. You can also take free courses on the internet on any subject you can imagine.

If you apply yourself for just one hour per day, in five years, you will be an expert in any field. Now, imagine giving two or three hours, daily, to a particular subject. Instead of watching movies and television in your spare time, why not use this time to learn and educate yourself. Read a book! Listen to audio messages in your chosen field. It is through your learning that your earning will increase. Turn your car into a university of learning instead of listening to the radio or music. Buy and read books. This is called self-investment.

To be educated in the Word of God is of more benefit than academic education. Word education will get you out of more problems than academic education will. Here is one thing you must realize about education: it is never too late to learn or be educated. So, do not use a lack of education as an excuse because you can educate yourself today.

BORN IN THE WRONG COUNTRY

Some people have disdain for their own nation. They think, "If only I could be in the U.S.A or England, then I will prosper." Certainly, America and the U.K are great nations. Yet, you were not born in the wrong country. You can succeed anywhere in the world. Your success is not dependent on your physical location. It is dependent on your spiritual and mental location. God told Joshua, "I will be with you. I will not fail thee nor forsake thee." (Joshua 1:5)

If God is on your side, what can the devil do? Romans 8:31 states, "What shall we then say to these things? If God be for us, who can be against us." Joseph, the dreamer, prospered and became the

Prime Minister in a place where he was not supposed to prosper. Why? Because God was with him. The same goes for Daniel. It does not matter where you were born. What matters is "as long as he sought the Lord, God made him to prosper" (2 Chronicles 26:5).

PAST EXPERIENCES

"Well, we've tried it before and we failed." So what! Do not let the past shape your future. What happened before is no indication that it will happen again.

Your past experiences do not determine your future potential and destiny. Winners are not those who never experience failure. Winners learned the right lesson and kept going – even after a setback. You cannot start the next chapter of your life if you keep rehashing your last one. Forget those things behind you and press onwards and upwards. If we are supposed to learn from experience then learn from your bad experiences and don't do what you did the last time. Yesterday's failure can become the springboard for tomorrow's success.

> You cannot start the next chapter of your life if you keep rehashing your last one.

UNDERSTANDING FAILURE

Allow me to help you understand failure. We, in the church, are afraid of the word "failure". The word "failure" has become bigger than the word "faith" for so many believers. They have the wrong concept of the word "failure". Because of this lack of understanding, whenever a person tastes failure, they take it personally. They ostracize themselves from the church body because of the stigma attached to the word "failure".

What is failure? It is the omission of expected or required action in the desired time. It is an act that you expected but for whatever

Chapter 4 • Seven Invalid Excuses

reason did not happen at the time you needed it. So, why take it personally? The reason we take it personally is because we think *we* are the failure. What you need to realize is that failure is an event and not a person. It is not you but something that you are going through.

Anyone who has ever achieved success in life has gone through failures. All failure is a learning curve. For example, when Thomas Edison was developing a commercially viable light bulb, he went through over ten thousand prototypes before he finally got it right.

> *I have not failed 10,000 times.* I have not failed once. I have succeeded in proving that those 10,000 ways will not work. When I have eliminated the ways that will not work, I will find the way that will work.
> – Thomas Edison

You, too, will eventually find a way that works. Don't take failure personally. I live my life with this simple little motto which will be helpful for you too: Never let success go to your head. In the same vein, never let failures go to your heart. If you do, you will be in big trouble.

Everyone fails at one time or another. When a baby learns to walk, he stumbles and falls. That does not make him a failure. It is just a phase he is going through. He gets up, staggers again, and holds on to something until he gets it right.

Have you ever had the wind knocked out of you? You felt despondent because of a "failure" only to learn later that it was not as bad as you felt? You have got to get up and keep plugging away until you get the desired result.

Don't give up at the first hurdle. Jump over it. Life is somewhat like the Olympic 110 meter hurdle, a hurdling track and field event for men. The female counterpart is the 100 meter hurdle. Ten hurdles of 1.067 meters (3.5 ft or 42 inches) in height are evenly spaced along a straight course of 110 meters. They are positioned so that they will fall over if bumped by the runner. Fallen hurdles, themselves, do not carry a penalty for the runners. However, they have a significant pull-over weight which slows down the runner. In the race of life, there will be hurdles to jump over. While they may not be the same height, if a hurdle exists, it can be jumped over.

I want you to notice this about the 110 meter hurdles, "They are positioned so that they will fall over if bumped by the runner." Any hurdle in your way will fall as you bump into them. Like Thomas Edison, I see failure as a learning curve. I do not let it become an issue in my life. I certainly will not allow an issue to become my identity. Unfortunately, this is what most people do. They allow an issue to become their identity. Never allow an issue to become your identity.

AGE

This is a big one that people use all the time. Some feel they are either too old or they are too young. While there can be some issues if one makes the mistake of stepping out too early. They can miss the correct timing. And, others can totally waste time. However, for the most part, people are still operating within the correct time frame. As you are reading this book, let me make this clear: You are neither too old nor too young. You are right on time. Moses was eighty years old when he began his ministry. Josiah was eight years old when he began ruling as king and did that which was right (2 Kings 22:1). You do not have any excuse. If Sarah had a child at ninety years old and Caleb could do battle at eighty-five years old, then you are not too old. This was Caleb's testimony:

> And now, behold, the LORD hath kept me alive, as he said, these forty and five years, even since the LORD spake this word unto Moses, while the children of Israel wandered in the wilderness: and now, lo, I am this

Chapter 4 • Seven Invalid Excuses

day fourscore and five years old. As yet I am as strong this day as I was in the day that Moses sent me: as my strength was then, even so is my strength now, for war, both to go out, and to come in. (Joshua 14:10-11)

You see, as long as you are focused, God will keep you strong. As long as Caleb was focused on his destiny, his strength was preserved. Moses was 120 years and was still strong and climbing up and down mountains. Do not make age an issue of the body when it is an issue of the mind. As a matter of fact, the older you become, the wiser and more experienced you should become. Now, you know what works and what does not work.

LACK OF SKILLS AND TALENTS

Not understanding the difference between talent and skill has caused people to think that those who are great achievers were super gifted people. Since not all are born with super gifts then not everyone can be successful. That's what some people think. However, nothing could be further from the truth. Talent has been defined as something that is natural to a person – something that is inherent or innate. A talent is also asserted as a special ability to do something without prior experience or tutelage. It is an instinctive flair to do such tasks effortlessly.

> Acquire special skills that can take you from mediocrity to excellence.

Skill, on the other hand, is what you have learned, practiced and developed over a period of time. A skill is an acquired ability as a result of constant, repeated action. Skill enables a desired performance and quicker result on a particular task. While not everybody is born with the same talent, everybody has the capacity to learn and earn a particular skill.

You may know people who are very talented. You may be thinking to yourself, "Hmm, I was not born with any special talent." That is not your problem. Talent can be limited to some people that not everybody is privy to. Yet, a skill can be learned and acquired by anyone who has the capacity, patience, time and willingness to learn. In essence, talent is natural ability and skill is acquired ability. While you may not have been born with any special talent, it is within your reach to acquire special skills that can take you from mediocrity to a life of excellence.

LACK OF MONEY

This may sound like a cliche´ but it is viable: "Provision follows vision." There is really no such thing as a lack of money. Money is all around you. There is money everywhere. As Dr. Robb Thompson has said many times, "Poverty is not the lack of money; poverty is the proof of misguided money." When someone says, "There is no money," what they mean is that person is facing personal lack.

No matter what the economy is doing, somebody, somewhere is making money. The key is to become a money magnet. Money is no respecter of persons. The problem is that they are following money when it should be the other way around.

Money should be following you. It can only do so if you are going somewhere and providing a service. Money will follow your dreams and visions. Look around you. People who are financially secure are those who had a dream, vision, idea and focus which empowered money to follow them. Look at Steve Jobs and Bill Gates. There is power in dreams and visions – spiritual, physical and financial power. Most people do not realize that's why the Holy Ghost came. They assume that the only reason He came was to give us tongues-power. That's true, but there's much more.

Chapter 4 • Seven Invalid Excuses

Peter and Joel gave us insight into the work of the Holy Spirit.

> *And it shall come to pass in the last days, saith God, I will pour out of my Spirit upon all flesh: and your sons and your daughters shall prophesy, and your young men shall see visions, and your old men shall dream dream.* (Acts 2:17)

The Holy Spirit came to activate visions and dreams in our lives. In Acts 1:8, Jesus said, "But ye shall receive power, after that the Holy Ghost is come upon you…"

The power is not only tongues-power but vision-power and dream-power. If there is no power and direction in your life, it is because you lack a dream or vision. If there is no spiritual power in your life, it is because you lack dreams and visions. Get a dream, be a dreamer and break out of your limitations.

PART II

KEYS TO FULFILLING YOUR DREAMS

THE VIRTUES AND VALUES OF GOAL SETTING

Chapter 5

For a dream cometh through the multitude of business... (Ecclesiastes 5:3a)

For the dream comes through much effort... (Ecclesiastes 5:3a NASB)

For a dream comes through much activity... (Ecclesiastes 5:3a NKJV)

For a dream comes with much business and painful effort... (Ecclesiastes 5:3a AMP)

In order for your dreams to be realized, you need to turn them into steps and actions. Sitting down will not lead you to see your dreams.

> *"And the LORD answered me, and said, Write the vision, and make it plain upon tables, that he may run that readeth it. For the vision is yet for an appointed time, but at the end it shall speak, and not lie: though it tarry, wait for it; because it will surely come, it will not tarry.* (Habakkuk 2:2-3)

Become a meaningful specific and not a wandering generality.

The wisdom of Solomon declared that you will have to get off your rear end. Employ your hands to activities in order to see the fulfillment of your dreams. The world says, "Good things come to those who wait". That is true in some instances. But, for your dreams to manifest, you will have to work. Good things come to those who work. Transforming desire into reality involves a process of goal setting and goal-related activity. The New King James Version puts it this way: "A dream comes through much activity." Embrace the following expressions of applying yourself to work:

- You will have to roll up your sleeves
- You will have to buckle down
- You will have to use some elbow grease

What are your dreams? Be specific. Know what you want. You have a specific purpose on the earth. You are on the earth to do something amazing with your life. While all humans have certain, general things in common, there is also something unique, distinct and specific about you. You will never realize more than a fraction of your potential as a wandering generality. I like how Zig Ziglar aptly stated it many years ago, "You must become a meaningful specific and not a wandering generality." It is a fact that people who have direction and purpose in their lives go further and faster. They get more done, in all areas of their lives. Here are some basic keys to fulfill your dreams.

HAVE A DREAM AND A VISION

Be a day-dreamer. Your dream must be your passion and obsession. You will not succeed at anything which is not your obsession. Everything starts with a dream and a vision. Before you can ever change your present circumstance, you have got to look at where you want to be. That is why a dream is important. Your dream or vision is where you want your life to go. Dreams give your life focus. They will cut out time wasting and give you a purpose and clear sense of direction. Your dreams suggest to people around you that you are going somewhere.

BE SPECIFIC

Earlier, you read this great quote – and it bears repeating: "Be a meaningful specific not a wandering generality." Know what you want. If you do not know what you want then nobody else will. No one can help you to get to where you are going if you, yourself, do not know where you are going. Have you ever heard this? "If you do not know where you are going then every road will take you there."

You were divinely created for a specific purpose. Find out what it is and go for it. Do not dabble into everything and specialize in nothing. It is said that if you do the same thing for one hour, on a daily basis, in five years you would be a specialist. Be someone specific! Be a specialist! Make your life count.

WRITE YOUR DREAM AND VISION

There is power in writing down your dreams and visions. When you write them down, you are making them concrete. Show me a man who does not write down his dreams and I will show you someone who easily forgets where he is going. When you write down your dreams, they help you not to stray away from your original intentions. It also helps people around you to be aware of your significance.

> *And the* LORD *answered me, and said, Write the vision, and make it plain upon tables, that he may run that readeth it.* (Habakkuk 2:2)

You need to have a book in which you write your dreams. Make them as extravagant as you want. It is your dream book! Dream as much as you want and as big as you want. Now, with the inventions of tablets and laptops, it's even easier to record things. You can have your dreams before you 24/7.

I have a notebook from 1990 in which I wrote my dreams and visions. Whenever I look at it, I see how far God has brought me. I have never thrown that notebook away. It reminds me of where I was, where I am today, and where I will be in the future. In this notebook, I had taped cut out clippings from magazines to visualize where I wanted to go. One of the dreams I had was to travel the world and preach the Gospel to the nations of the world.

The first time I traveled to Nigeria, on British Airways, I picked up the airline's in-flight magazine. In it, they had a page detailing all the routes that airline flew. I cut that page out and put it in my dream notebook. At the time, I was living in London and operated from it as a base. It made total sense to me to have a page, in my dream book, with arrows pointing from London to different parts of the world. It was a perfect visual of my dream. God has been faithful and enabled me to travel the world. Now, I have television and radio pictures in my dream book, depicting that I see myself as a voice to the media.

> People who have direction and purpose go further and faster.

THE VALUES AND VIRTUES OF SETTING GOALS

Once you have a specific dream and you have written it down, it becomes imperative that you understand the value and virtue of setting goals. This is extremely important if you want to take your dreams from the invisible to the visible realm. You must apply and begin to activate the secrets of goal setting. Anyone who has had a major impact in the earth has tapped into the secret of goal setting.

> *One thing have I desired of the LORD, that will I seek after; that I may dwell in the house of the LORD all the days of my life, to behold the beauty of the LORD, and to enquire in his temple. (Psalm 27:4)*

I want you to notice these tremendous words, "One thing have I desired that I will seek after" meaning one goal that I have and I will seek after. Replace the word *desire* with the word *goal*. This verse can be written as, "one goal or desire that I have and that I will seek after." Psalm 27:4 can be translated as, "One thing have I desired, or one goal is what I have of the Lord and that will I seek after."

The act of goal setting will change your destiny. It will be the master key to success in life. Although the words "goals, dreams, desires,

Chapter 5 • The Virtues and Values of Goal Setting

wishes and visions" are somewhat similar, they are very distinct. A dream or a vision is the big picture of where you want to go. If no complimentary actions and time schedule are attached to it, then, it is merely a wish. A wish is something you would like to have but are not willing to pay the price for nor put in the time to obtain. Let us look at a few more differences between a goal, a desire, a wish and a vision.

> *The soul of the sluggard desireth, and hath nothing: but the soul of the diligent shall be made fat.* (Proverbs 13:4)

Notice that both the sluggard and the diligent have desires. Only the diligent obtains his desire because he has a different mindset than the sluggard. I want to look at this verse from several translations of the Bible:

> *Indolence wants it all and gets nothing; the energetic have something to show for their lives.* (The Message)

> *Lazy people want much but get little, but those who work hard will prosper* (NLT)

> *Lazy people always want things but never get them. Those who work hard get plenty.* (ERV)

Here, you have the sluggard and the diligent. You have the competent and those who are incompetent. Both have desires, but only one of them fulfills their desires.

> *Hope deferred maketh the heart sick: but when the desire cometh, it is a tree of life.* (Proverbs 13:12)

Notice something here: there are desires that stay in the realm of desires. The book of Proverbs is telling you that your desire can come from the realm of the spirit and be actualized. Your desire can move from the realm of the invisible to the realm of the visible. When the desire comes, it is a tree of life. Just as the tree of life, in Eden, would have given life to Adam – had he partaken of it – a tree of life gives life to a person. The fulfillment and accomplishment of your dream will enthuse energy, zest and joy into your life.

The desire accomplished is sweet to the soul: but it is abomination to fools to depart from evil. (Proverbs 13:19)

According to those two verses, a desire can come and be accomplished. In today's vernacular, if something good has happened to someone, they say, "That's sweet man, sweet!" If somebody gave you $1,000 you would say, "Sweet! Praise God". Many cannot employ the word "Sweet" in their vocabulary because their desires have not been accomplished. What is the problem? The problem is that the desire is staying in the realm of desire, and never materializing. Why?

Let's go back to Psalms 27:4 which reads, "One thing have I desired, or one goal is what I have of the Lord and that will I seek after." Your desire cannot materialize unless you pursue it. Many years ago, Mike Murdock stated that the proof of desire is pursuit. If the proof of desire is pursuit, then the proof of pursuit is progress. The only way you can gauge that you are rightly pursuing after your desire is if you see progress.

If your dream is to weigh under 200 pounds and fit in a size 32 jeans and you are presently a size 38 waist, the only way you can properly gauge progress in your pursuit is if your size 38 pants are becoming loose. Now, if your size 38 pants are getting tighter, that would indicate that there has been no progress in the pursuit of your dream.

Another reason our desires have not materialized – and we cannot say 'sweet" – is we have never attached goals to them. If your desire does not have a goal attached to it, then what you have is merely wishful thinking. We are going to look into why people do not set goals. More importantly, why have *you* not attached goals to *your* dreams?

Chapter 5 ● The Virtues and Values of Goal Setting

CLASSIFICATIONS OF GOALS

Goal setting is the infrastructure upon which personal, spiritual or professional achievements are built. Without goal setting, you have no infrastructure to build a life of super achievements. It is the scaffolding for the building and erecting of your dream. You cannot build anything without infrastructure.

Goal setting is a road map – your GPS – to your destiny. Not having any goals is leaving your life to time and chance. You do not want to leave your life to happenstance. When you do not set any goals, your life is at the mercy of others. When you start to have goals, you become in charge of your life. Let me reiterate this thought, "Your ability to set goals is your master skill to success." To be goalless is to roam aimlessly on the earth. It is like sailing without a compass. You will not be going anywhere specific. You will be like a ship at sea without a rudder. You will just be drifting all over the place.

Goal setting is the gauge to measure progress or stagnancy. Are progressing or regressing. Are you moving forward or backward? Most people cannot tell if their lives, ministry and business have moved forward. You have got to have some kind of gauge to help you measure how far you have come. If you do not know how far you have progressed, how will you be able to make the proper adjustments.

> Without goal setting, you have no infrastructure to build a life of super achievements.

A goal is what you want to achieve in a given period of time

This is to be your primary definition of goals. People have said, "A goal is what I'm aiming for". That is too weak and too vague. You see, there are people who have aimed for something and never gotten it. Why? Because there were no specifics attached to it. This is why you must get a proper concept of what a goal is. It is what you want to achieve in a given period of time.

There is no point in screaming, "I want to lose weight. I want to lose weight!" People say that all the time and never lose weight. The specific should be, "By when?" How much weight do you want to lose? You have got to firmly grasp this: For a goal to be a goal, it has to have a time limit. You have to have a time schedule! Say, "By *this* time I am going to achieve *this*."

For example, you could say, "I am going to lose 10 lbs in four weeks." If there is no time element involved, you will just be drifting in the sea of vagueness. You won't begin to exercise or make a change to your eating habits. Hence, you will not see a change.

A goal is your anticipated result, guiding your actions and reactions

A goal is an end that one strives to attain. It is the end towards which effort is directed. For your goals to be fulfilled, your actions and reactions must be complimentary to anticipated results. Goals do not achieve themselves by themselves. There has to be some effort directed toward the fulfillment of that goal.

A goal is a demand for action

> *For a dream cometh through the multitude of business...* (Ecclesiastes 5:3a)

The Amplified® Bible renders this verse as, "For a dream comes with much business and painful effort." There have to be some activities, a multitude of business and plenty of actions. You cannot stay in your comfort zone. The moment you set a specificity of time, it will force you to work. What do I mean by work? It means, "Sustained physical and mental effort to overcome obstacles to achieve an objective, thereby securing results." What are you working on? What do you want to achieve? What activities have you done?

Your goal setting ability puts you on the runway to achievement and success. Irrespective of your age, you must have goals for your life.

Chapter 5 ● The Virtues and Values of Goal Setting

I am sure this is not the first time you have heard about setting goals. So, why is it that so many people do not set goals?

A while ago, a study was done. We will crunch the numbers to fit today's growing population. We have over 7 billion people populating the earth. For a long time, statistics showed that only about 10% set goals. That 10% would also have to include a few Christians who have goals. Out of the 10%, only about 3% take the time to consciously sit and write down their goals down. Now, the updated statistics are showing that only 3% of the world population sets goals. Are you in the 90+% who do not have goals? Will you be part of the minimal percentage of people who not only have written a goal but have taken action – as well as reaction – toward their goals? Will you relentlessly pursue your goals?

Now, putting aside the percentage of world population who sets goals, let us look at Christendom. The figures are even more alarming. By Christendom, I am referring to the worldwide body or society of Christians. That includes all the denominations in the world. Less than 5% of Christians write down and set goals. Is it any wonder that a lot of believers do not achieve much in their lives?

A lot of believers are just drifting in life, waiting for death or the Resurrection. They are not living life to their fullest potential. What they do not understand is that God, Himself, is a goal oriented Person. Jesus was a goal oriented Person. What Jesus achieved in three and a half years would have taken some people two lifetimes, if not more. John, in his Gospel, wrote:

> And Jesus did such a number of other things that, if every one was recorded, it is my opinion that even the world itself is not great enough for the books there would be. (John 21:25 BBE)

Jesus was a high achiever to the highest degree. He had one major goal when He arrived and that was to save humanity (John 3:16).

He was relentlessly focused on His goal. He did not tolerate distractions and severely rebuked even one of His closest allies, Peter, who tried to dissuade Him from His purpose (Mathew 16:20-24). See how focused Jesus was? Luke penned these words to Theophilus in his first treatise:

> And it came to pass, when the time was come that he should be received up, he stedfastly set his face to go to Jerusalem. (Luke 9:51)

The Prophet Isaiah said, "He set his face like a flint…" (Isaiah 50:7) When you are a person with goals, you are a highly focused person.

> Looking unto Jesus the author and finisher of our faith; who for the joy that was set before him endured the cross, despising the shame, and is set down at the right hand of the throne of God. (Hebrews 12:2)

"For God so loved the world that he gave his only begotten Son…" What was God's purpose or goal for putting Jesus on the earth? To save the world. So, God is a goal oriented Person. Your Savior and your Redeemer, is goal oriented.

In the beginning, God said, "Let us make man in our image and after our likeness and let them have dominion." Therefore, if God is goal oriented then you need to be goal oriented. This is one of the ways to dominate in the earth. You have got to be driven by goals.

Do not allow yourself to get so busy that you do not have time to think about goals. Do not allow life to make you so busy that you focus on the present and try to reshape your past but don't have time to think about your future. Without exception, everybody has 365 days a year, 7 days a week and 24 hours in one day. It is what you do daily with your 24 hours, every day, that will determine what you will acquire.

What are you working on?

WHY PEOPLE DO NOT SET GOALS

Chapter 6

To live a goalless life is to roam aimlessly in the earth. As important and biblical as goal setting is, millions of people and believers have not realized the virtues and values of it. Consequently, they never apply themselves to this powerful secret to success. I am going to list ten reasons why people do not set goals.

> It will take goal setting to fulfill the will of God.

1. Because goal setting is considered to be unspiritual.

Many Christians do not set goals because somehow they deem that goal setting as "unspiritual." Especially in the Charismatic and Pentecostal circles, we feel that it is irrelevant to our lives. We escape setting goals by saying, "I am led by the Spirit" or "I am waiting on God". While I totally believe in the leading of the Spirit, most believers have cognitive dissonance when it comes to goal setting. What is cognitive dissonance? It is the state of having inconsistent thoughts, beliefs, or attitudes as it pertains to behavioral decisions and attitude changes. It is a mental clash of the old program with new software. In other words, the car is still in reverse yet you want to go forward. It will never happen. For whatever reason – and a complete lack of teaching – the church has earmarked goal setting as a worldly work of the flesh. It is viewed as relying upon the flesh rather than God. Yet, the Apostle Paul, who taught us about the leading of the Spirit, was a goal oriented person.

Paul planted many churches, wrote two thirds of the New Testament, went on three missionary journeys – covering thousands of miles without modern transportation – and led thousands to Jesus. How did he and other biblical characters accomplish so much in their lives and walk with God? They set goals. Goal setting is very spiritual. Paul said to the Philippian saints, "I press toward the mark for the prize of the high calling of God in Christ Jesus" (Philippians 3:14). In fact, I like many of the modern translations of this verse:

> *I pursue as my goal the prize promised by God's heavenly call in Christ Jesus.* (HCSB)
>
> *I keep pursuing the goal to win the prize of God's heavenly call in the Messiah Jesus.* (ISV)
>
> *With this goal in mind, I strive toward the prize of the upward call of God in Christ Jesus.* (NET)
>
> *And I run toward the goal to take the victory of the calling of God from on high in Yeshua The Messiah.* (ARAM)
>
> *I run straight toward the goal to win the prize that God's heavenly call offers in Christ Jesus.* (GW)

While the King James Version uses "mark", the newer translations employ the word "goal". The Greek word for "mark" is the word *skopos* from which we derive our English word 'scope". *Strong's Concordance* pictures a sentry keeping guard over a place, looking through a scope, intently, at a target in the distance.

The problem is many believers think there is a discrepancy between goal setting and the will of God. It is viewed as somehow negating or aborting the will of God. In contrast, the Bible shows us that it will take goal setting to *fulfill* the will of God. Nehemiah, knowing the will of God, had a specific goal and a specific time frame to rebuild the wall of Jerusalem. He did it in 52 days. The will of God was revealed to David that the temple of God needed to be built. However it would be Solomon whom God said would build the temple as David had blood on his hands. With a clear cut goal, it took Solomon seven years to finish the

Chapter 6 • Why People Do Not Set Goals

temple of God. Goal setting causes you to be a focused planner. God, Himself, is a planner and goal oriented. See what Paul says to the Ephesians:

> *He [God] planned to bring all of history to its goal in Christ. Then Christ would be the head of everything in heaven and on earth.*
> (Ephesians 1:10 GW)

Therefore, I need you to understand that there is unity between the will of God, spirituality and goal setting. Let us allow Paul to have the final word on this matter,

> *So I do not run without a goal. I fight like a boxer who is hitting something—not just the air.* (1 Corinthians 9:26 NSV)

2. Because of their upbringing.

Many people grew up in a household where goal setting was not a priority. They grew up with goal deficient parents. For some parents, sending their children to school was not for the betterment of the child but rather to get them out of the house and out of their hair for seven hours. Many children grew up with parents who were not driven to succeed; they lived mediocre lives. Many grew up with parents who never read books, but watched television all day long. Achievement and the art of goal setting were no where near their vicinity. Therefore, if a child grows up in that environment, it is only logical that goal setting is not a must in his life.

Fortunately, my parents were driven to succeed in life irrespective of their education levels. I was also blessed to go to a Christian school that taught us to set goals for the day's work and study.

3. Because they don't know *how* to set goals.

In a way, this is somewhat of a plausible excuse for many. How can you do something if you do not know how to do it? Many did not go to schools where goal setting was taught in class. You can go through your primary, secondary, high school and college without ever being taught how to have and set goals. Yet, if you were to ask any great achiever what their main key to success was, you will hear "setting goals". Because of ignorance in goal setting, some people set too big a goal and later become discouraged.

4. Because of fear of failure due to past experience.

A bad experience or seeing someone else who failed in their goal setting endeavor has put a damper on too many. To fail at something or to see someone close to you fail can leave an indelible mark on a person. Failure can leave a mark, spiritually, psychologically, physically and socially. Some people take failure personally – as a form of rejection and as an end.

People do not understand that there is a difference between failure and an ailment. A failure is something that happens to you from the outside. An ailment is something that occurs from the inside. Failure is not a final foe but the voice of correction. Failures will be part of the journey, so don't take failure personally. It means you have hit a learning curve.

Thomas Edison, the inventor of the light bulb, had done over 10,000 experiments before he got it right. Failure taught him what worked and what did not work. Failure is an event, not a person. It is a phase you are going through but not who you are.

> The moment you start looking at failure from a point of education rather than rejection you will begin to thrive on it.

Success means you have mastered the learning curve. The moment you start looking at failure from a point of education rather than rejection, you will begin to thrive in it. Most people see failure as rejection of themselves. Every highly successful person and achiever have tasted failure. However, they still came out on top because they did not take it personally. They just took it as a learning curve.

Chapter 6 • Why People Do Not Set Goals

5. Because of the fear of criticism and ridicule.

This can swing in two ways. Some people feel that if they do not achieve a set goal, other people will criticize or ridicule them. Others are afraid that once they attempt to achieve a goal, people will criticize and mock them. When Joseph announced his dream, his brothers grew angry with him and eventually sold him into slavery to get rid of him. While Jacob, his father, was attentive to his dream, his brothers were plotting his death. While Potiphar exalted him, Potiphar's wife was plotting his demise.

The life of Joseph teaches us that you should not share your dreams and goals with any and every one. Never reveal your goals to naysayers and negative people. Only share with those who will celebrate and assist you in your endeavors. Better still, let people know by your results, achievements and accomplishments – after the fact.

Equally important is to never be afraid of other people's criticism. People criticize because they have limited understanding. Don't let other people's ridicule stop you. Simply set your goals and run hard after them. You cannot let the voice of other people determine the direction of your life.

> *But instead of spending our lives running towards our dreams, we are often running away from a fear of failure or a fear of criticism.*
> –Eric Wright

6. Because they are satisfied with the status quo.

People do not set goals because they are OK with the here and now. They are satisfied to be in their comfort zone, with what they have and where they are in life. So, they do not want to push for greatness. You see, achievement and greatness will force you out of the status quo. Nothing will ever change without you getting mad at your present situation. As long as you can put up with it, you will stay in it.

Goal setting will demand that you get out of your comfort zone. Research has shown us that there are only two motivating factors which cause people to change: pain and pleasure. As long as people are satisfied with the status quo, they will not explore what else is available or what greater things they could achieve. A "status quo" mindset is backward thinking. It is cementing your life and mindset in the past.

7. Because they are not ambitious, driven, nor hungry enough.

This is a fact: some people do not set goals because they are just not driven enough or ambitious enough. They lack the inner desire to do or want something greater than what they currently have. I have discovered that some people are happy with the ordinary. Are you hungry for success? When Mike Tyson was hungry, ambitious and driven, he was successful. He became the heavyweight champion of the world. When comfort and wealth set in, he lost his hunger and drive for success. You have got to be hungry, driven and ambitious. Those who are hungry will stop at nothing. They are like a hungry lion in search of a prey. They won't back down until their hunger is satisfied.

Allow me to pose some questions to you?
- Do you still possess a "Yes I can" mentality?
- Are you hungry for impact upon the earth?
- Are you hungry enough to reinvent yourself?
- Are you ambitious enough to grow and break out beyond your present life?
- Are you too driven to disallow pessimism, obstacles, denials and delays to stop your forward movement?

Those who are hungry and driven will stop at nothing to fulfill their life's destiny.

8. Because they feel overwhelmed by life, too busy and it would be an additional ordeal.

Some people are like the hamster – spinning his wheel but not going anywhere in life. There are people whose lives are busy but producing very little. The old idiom, "to have one's finger in too many pies," rings true for many. Much of what they are involved in is viewed as major when in reality they are minor things. In their busy-ness, the thought of goal setting makes them feel overwhelmed. There is a deception in thinking that mere busy-ness is productivity. That is not always the case. Some people have said, "I am too busy to set goals. I do not have time for this." What they don't realize is that goal setting will de-clutter their life and allow them to focus on what is most important.

Many times, people feel overwhelmed because they have not learned to say, "No". You have to learn to say "No" without feeling guilty. Just say "No" or you will constantly be pulled in different directions. Achievers have mastered the skill of eliminating distractions from their lives in order to give total focus on what they are endeavoring to achieve.

Time is not something you have the luxury of wasting – it is your scarcest resource. If you feel so overwhelmed, it is probably because you have your finger in too many pies. Therefore, you have to get some stuff off of your plate and focus upon that which is major.

> Failure is not a final foe but the voice of correction.

9. Because they are disorganized and don't want to change.

Disorganization is the mother of disorder and non-productivity. Find someone who is disorganized and you will find someone who is not keen on goal setting. Some will use the excuse that goal setting will cramp their spontaneous personality. Actually, what many people call spontaneity is disorder. Goal setting, when fully implemented, will force you to be organized or orderly. Being orderly is the key to productivity. One of the ways to be orderly is to start with goal setting.

10. Because they are lazy.
Lazy people do not set goals. Laziness is defined as the quality of being unwilling to work or use energy. A person may have an understanding of the virtues and values of goal setting and still not act upon that understanding. That is what laziness is. It is knowing the facts but not having the desire to apply energy to them.

A long time ago, I heard a statement which made a huge impact upon me: "If you want to have great finances then you have to learn to be in the top 10% of your field." I strive for this; how about you? Are you in the top 10% of your field? You have got to learn how to be in the top 10% of your field. That is what pushes me to read so much and study so much, even if I don't feel like it. Some days, I do not feel like studying and striving. There are days in which I do not feel like praying and fasting? I would just love to just coast through life, sometimes. I have discovered that one day of coasting can become one week of coasting – then one month. Then, it becomes a habit and a lifestyle. Laziness is a lifestyle habit.

Your goals will demand you to break laziness in your life. The Bible has some great remarks on laziness. How can you tell when someone is lazy? Let me list ten characteristics:

1. The lazy is a know-it-all.

    The sluggard is wiser in his own conceit than seven men that can render a reason. (Proverbs 26:16)

2. The lazy will not finish what he started. The lazy has no stickability.

The slothful man roasteth not that which he took in hunting: but the substance of a diligent man is precious. (Proverbs 12:27)

3. The lazy is a waster.

   He also that is slothful in his work is brother to him that is a great waster. (Proverbs 18:9)

4. The lazy is negligent.

   I went by the field of the slothful, and by the vineyard of the man void of understanding; And, lo, it was all grown over with thorns, and nettles had covered the face thereof, and the stone wall thereof was broken down. (Proverbs 24:30-31)

5. The lazy refuses to work.

   A slothful man hideth his hand in his bosom, and will not so much as bring it to his mouth again. (Proverbs 19:24)

   The desire of the slothful killeth him; for his hands refuse to labour. (Proverbs 21:25)

6. The lazy is full of excuses.

   The slothful man saith, There is a lion without, I shall be slain in the streets. (Proverbs 22:13)

7. The lazy is vexatious and irritating.

   As vinegar to the teeth, and as smoke to the eyes, so is the sluggard to them that send him. (Proverbs 10:26)

8. The lazy is void of understanding.

   And, lo, it was all grown over with thorns, and nettles had covered the face thereof, and the stone wall thereof was broken down. Then I saw, and considered it well: I looked upon it, and received instruction. Yet a little sleep, a little slumber, a little folding of the hands to sleep: So shall thy poverty come as one that travelleth; and thy want as an armed man. (Proverbs 24:30-34)

9. The lazy has desire but will not see the fulfillment.

   The soul of the sluggard desireth, and hath nothing: but the soul of the diligent shall be made fat. (Proverbs 13:4)

10. The lazy substitutes hard work with get rich quick schemes.

    He that tilleth his land shall have plenty of bread: but he that followeth after vain persons shall have poverty enough. (Proverbs 28:19)

DIVERSITIES, TYPES AND CLASSIFICATIONS OF GOALS

Chapter 7

By now, I hope you understand the values and the virtues of goal setting. It is important for you, as a believer, to grasp this great secret to success. We have seen that in order for your dreams or desires to materialize, they need to be turned into goals. For something to be considered a desire, there has to be a pursuit. If there is no pursuit of the desire then it is merely wishful thinking. You must understand that in order to reach your destiny, it is imperative to have goals.

> Your ignorance gives your enemy an unfair advantage over your life.

To be goalless in life, is to roam about aimlessly on earth. If you don't have goals in life, you have no gauge by which to measure progression or regression. How do you get from point A to point B? As already mentioned, a great key will be "goals". This is the reason it is important for you to know and understand the ins and outs of goals. We have discovered that one of the major reasons people do not set goals is because they do not know how to. The world says that "ignorance is bliss". The Word disagrees:

> *My people are destroyed for lack of knowledge: because thou hast rejected knowledge, I will also reject thee, that thou shalt be no priest to me: seeing thou hast forgotten the law of thy God, I will also forget thy children* (Hosea 4:6).

You see, your ignorance is the strength of your enemy. It gives him an unfair advantage over your life. It is, therefore, required that you know the diversities, types and classifications of goals in order for you to successfully attain them.

THE DIVERSITIES OF GOALS

Life is lived at different stages and on different levels. What is a goal for a retired person may not be a goal for a college student. Therefore goals adjust to time, stages, environment and age. According to the Apostle Paul, man is a tripartite being composed of spirit, soul and body. Therefore, you will need to have goals for each area.

We know that the soul is comprised of the mind, will and emotions; the body is made up of your flesh with which you relate in the earth. Your physical being delves into a myriad of activities such as working, marrying, vacationing and exercising, to name a few. As you can glean, your life has diverse functions. You will need to have specific goals for each, respective aspect of your life. So, let us look at some of the common diversities of life:

1. Spiritual

Do you have a plan to be spiritually strong? Have you decided how many hours you will pray daily? How many days will you fast weekly and yearly? How will you be strong spiritually? What convention and seminar will you attend? What church are you attending? Is it the one that is close to your house but does not feed or challenge you spiritually? You will not grow spiritually by happenstance. It has to be a goal and a purpose driven action.

2. Mental

Are you mentally strong or do you fall apart at the slightest problem? Do you have mental toughness or do you run and hide, bury your head in the sand – like an ostrich – and hope the problem will vanish? How many books will you read weekly? What and how many messages will you listen to in order to renew your mind and give you fresh insight? These have to be deliberate acts. It will not happen haphazardly.

3. Physical

What is your ideal weight this year? Are you joining a gym? Are you walking or running? Have you cut down on or eliminated junk food? Do not blame hereditary factors for your size. A lot of it is your mouth! What are you doing daily to reach your ideal weight? How is your health? How will your daily routine and eating habits affect you ten years down the road?

4. Professional

What is your ideal job? Do you want to run your own business? Have you developed the necessary skills and knowledge to be in the top 10% of your field? Are you missed when you are absent? Where will you be, professionally, five years down the road? Are you looking for promotion? Is there a management position you can apply for? Do you have to apply yourself to get the management position? Are you obtaining the necessary knowledge, skills and abilities to make yourself a viable candidate – or do you just want to be one of the boys?

5. Financial

How much money do you want to make this year? How much are you going to give this year? How much do you plan to save this year? Are there any investment plans? Are you in debt? If so, what is the plan to pay it off? If you do not have a plan to pay off a debt, as quickly as you can, the interest will rob you of future finances that you should have been enjoying. If you do not have a goal for your finances then you could be stuck on a fixed income. The way to break out of a fixed income is to have financial goals.

6. Relational

Have you evaluated the relationships in your life? Are you being loyal to people who are detrimental to your future and destiny? Are you fostering new relationships that will take you to your desired destination? If not, why not? Are there some relationships that you need to cut off and some that you need to pursue? Do what you have to do and stop procrastinating because of emotional ties.

7. Recreational

When was the last time you took a vacation? When was the last time that you, your spouse and your kids had fun together for a week? Have you been anywhere lately or are you just going to work and church and back? Some people's lives revolve around just work and church? You need time to unwind. You have to set a goal to go on vacation. The reason you have not gone on vacation is not necessarily because you cannot afford to. It has not been a goal and a plan.

8 Marital

Are you married? What are your goals for your marriage this year? Most couples stop courting after they are married. They let themselves go. Excitement and romance are gone after marriage. Do you have plans to be with your spouse? When was the last time you and your spouse went on a date or went to the restaurant by yourselves without the kids? You need to rekindle the flame of passion in your marriage. Having a great marriage is not automatic; it is something that you must continually strive for.

9. Familial

Do you have a close family or are the relationships fragmented? Do you have an ideal family or do you tolerate one another and cannot wait to get away from them? Is a family reunion a pleasure to look forward to or do you hate family reunions? How is your relationship with your children? Do you have family time? I do not just mean going to church together, as great as that is. Do you have vacation time together? Do you play games together? Do you have fun time together? You have to have goals for your family to be close, strong

Chapter 7 • Diversities, Types and Classifications of Goals

and knitted together. Living in the same house does not necessarily mean living in harmony.

10. Pensional

You may be in the sun season of your life now but a time is coming when you will be in the moon season of your life. What are you doing today that will take care of you in your later years? Will you be looking for a handout from your children and family or do you have investments that you will be able to draw from? What kind of retirement goals do you have? Have you thought about how much money you will need? Will your house be paid off? Do you have an inheritance plan for your children or will you leave them with a funeral bill? Do you have life insurance? I know many think that living by faith means you do not need any of these? Actually that kind of mentality is foolishness. Living by faith does not mean being irresponsible and stupid! What many call faith is irresponsibility. You cannot say, "Because I live by faith, I do not need home insurance or building insurance!" First of all, it would be illegal and the system will come down on you. Now, if you can have home or building insurance, why not have life insurance to take care of the physical building you live in?

CLASSIFICATION OF GOALS

Remember, a goal is what you want to achieve in a given amount of time. What makes a goal valid is taking it out of the realm of generality and making it specific. What makes it specific is that you put a time limit on it. A goal is your anticipated result. It's an end you strive to attain, toward which your effort and energy are directed. When your goals are time framed, it suggests the end is in view. Since time limits render a goal concrete, let us look at the classifications of goals to give us a better perspective:
- Long term goal

- Medium term goal
- Short term goal
- Immediate goal

AN IMPORTANT POINT

Before we define the different classifications, allow me to give you an overview – and make a very important point. Your long term goal is the main objective you want to achieve in your life. It is your life goal and can also been called your life achievement goal. However, to achieve your long term goal, you will have to fulfill the medium term goal. In order to do that, you have to set short term goals. You cannot fulfill the short term goal unless you meet the immediate or pressing goal. They correlate with one another. In other words, you set immediate or pressing goals in order to achieve your short term goals. That, in turn, is the stepping stone to fulfill the medium term goal. Having done so, you now have the infrastructure to fulfill your life goal – also known as your long term goal. Therefore, the important point is that although we list the long term as your ultimate or life goal it is not automatically fulfilled. It needs the sequence of immediate, short term and medium term to be the fulfilling bedrock for the long term goal achievement. In a nutshell, you set immediate goals to fulfill short term goals. You set short term goals in order to fulfill medium term goals and you set medium term goals in order to fulfill long term goals.

Long Term: 10-25 Years

A long term goal is something you want to achieve in the long run, better known as the future. Long-term goals are important for a successful life and career. A long term goal is not something you can do this week or even this year. A long term goal will be a life achievement goal – your main focus and what you want to be remembered for. That is why long term goals usually take ten to

Chapter 7 • Diversities, Types and Classifications of Goals

twenty years to achieve; sometimes, they can take even longer. It is not something you can finish in one day, one week, one year or even five years. It is the big picture or the grand scheme of your life. It will take many steps to complete a long-term goal. These smaller steps will be your short-term and medium term goals.

Medium Term: 5-10 Years

A medium term goal will be the springboard upon which you can leap to your long term goal. It will be the bridge for the achievement of your long term goal. The medium term goals are usually longer than one year but will not go beyond ten years. They can usually be met between five and ten years. It is the leverage goal upon which you can build your life. Therefore, you must always keep an eye on it, making sure that you are moving in the right direction and at the right pace.

Short Term: 1-5 Years

Experts have stated that a short-term goal is something that will take at least a year to accomplish. Short term goals can range between one and five years. These are the foundational goals that will enable completion of the medium to long term goals. It is the small things that make the difference. It is what you want to happen in the near future. You must keep in mind that just as a building can be no stronger than its foundation, your long term goals will not be met without the achievement of short term goals.

Immediate Term: Daily/Weekly/Monthly

This is what gets the ball rolling. Without the immediate or pressing goals, you are procrastinating. It is what you do, daily, that will determine what you experience in five, ten and twenty years. Achieving pressing goals will enable you to reach your short-term goals. In turn, it will give you the ability to achieve your medium term goals which

Immediate Goals
+ Short Term
+ Medium Term
+ Long Term Goals
= Destiny

will, in turn, give you the power and strength to complete your long term goals. You need to work on your daily goals in order to set an infrastructure to achieve your long term goals. In order to complete the big picture, you need to start somewhere. Start with the here and now goals. It is important for us to grasp these four classifications of goals.

THE ONE CRITERIA YOU NEED TO KNOW

We have seen the diversities of goals. We have also understood the classifications of goals. We have gone through the values and virtues of goals. Yet, with all this knowledge, one can still fail in "goals". What is the most important criteria that makes "goals" viable? If goal setting was a straight forward, automatic deal, then everybody who ever delved into it would be highly successful. As you know, this is not reality. This is why many are cynical about goals.

If goal setting is such a powerful and positive phenomenon, then why is it that most people, who set out to achieve some kind of goal, fail? How can such a powerful tool become an abject fear or resistance for many? It all boils down to a lack of knowledge. When goals are not set correctly, they become more of a stumbling block than a way maker. What do we mean by not setting goal correctly? To put it plainly, some people, in their hyped up enthusiasm, simply set unrealistic goals that are just not feasible.

> Living by faith does not mean being irresponsible and stupid.

An unrealistic goal is like trying to get to the moon without a space ship. It is just not going to happen! Some people think that if they set an unachievable goal somehow this will enhance their reputation. In most cases, this only leads to total frustration and failure. This is where we have to apply the SMART goal principle. The SMART

goal principle will expose what an unrealistic goal is. You need to fully grasp this concept. SMART is an acronym:
- **S** – Specific
- **M** – Measurable
- **A** – Attainable
- **R** – Realistic
- **T** – Time Bound

S – Specific

Set specific goals – nothing vague, broad or general. Vague goals create vague results. Know exactly what you are shooting for. A goal that is well defined will give clarity, direction and focus. The moment you focus on a goal, it becomes like a magnet, pulling you and the necessary resources toward it. A specific goal will answer the following six questions:

1. **Who** will be the personnel involved? Your goals will need assistance.
2. **What** exactly do you want to accomplish?
3. **Where** is this happening? Identify a location. Placement and positioning are extremely important.
4. **When** will this happen? Establish a time frame. If you do not, you will flounder in procrastination and delaying tactics.
5. **Which** requirements and constraints are in play? Which skills do I need? What don't I have? Which habits do I need to implement in my life? Which people do I need to walk away from?
6. **Why** am I doing this? What are the specific reasons for accomplishing the goal.

M – Measurable

Some goals are easy to measure such as weight loss or income; others are a bit more difficult. Being able to track progress is an incentive to push further. You need to establish concrete criteria for measuring progress. A goal without a measurable mechanism or measurable conclusion is like playing sports without a scoreboard or scorekeeper.

A – Attainable

Stretch for it! You will not attain what you do not strive for. Your goal will need to stretch you... not break you. It will demand that you are action oriented. Action gives traction.

R – Realistic

An unrealistic goal is an unreachable goal. By realistic, I mean that the goal must be relevant and real to you. A realistic goal is one toward which you are both willing and able to work and commit. Some people set such unreasonably lofty goals. Even as they are setting it, in their minds, they know they will not be able to fulfill its obligations. That does not mean that you should set low goals. A goal can be both high and realistic. You are the determining factor on whether your goal is realistic or unrealistic, high or low.

T – Time Based

There must be a deadline. This is what separates a goal from a mere wish. Time bound goals will be the difference between success and mediocrity in your life. Putting a deadline – a finish line or an expiration date – on a particular goal gives you a clear target to work towards. When there is no time frame, there will be no sense of urgency. Procrastination will be the order of the day. A time bound goal is what will eliminate procrastination and time wasting.

The SMART goal principle will teach you how to set goals correctly and keep you on track for their successful execution.

PLAN OF ACTION AND TIME MANAGEMENT

Chapter 8

In order for our dreams to be turned into realities, we must turn them into goals. More specifically, we must turn them into SMART goals. Now, having this understanding will do you no good if you do not strategize your time, movements and activities accordingly.

> Dreams coupled with actions become realities.

BE COMMITTED TO YOUR DREAMS

It is great that you have a dream; it is better for your dream to have you. If you are not committed to your dreams, then your dreams will not be committed to you. If you are not committed to your dreams, then nobody else will be committed to them.

One thing is for sure: your dream will be challenged. No matter the challenge, you must pursue your dreams, relentlessly. Don't ever quit on your dreams. Many people have, and they lived to regret it. One bad decision can wreck your life. So, follow your dreams through. God is not impressed with starters but with finishers. The Scripture clearly reveals to us that God loves finishers.

- God finished the heavens and the earth

  Thus the heavens and the earth were finished, and all the host of them. And on the seventh day God ended his work which he had made; and he rested on the seventh day from all his work which he had made. And God blessed the seventh day, and sanctified it: because that in it he had rested from all his work which God created and made. (Genesis 2:1-3)

- Noah finished the ark

  Thus did Noah; according to all that God commanded him, so did he. (Genesis 6:22)

- Moses finished the tabernacle

  And he reared up the court round about the tabernacle and the altar, and set up the hanging of the court gate. So Moses finished the work. (Exodus 40:33)

- Moses finished writing the Book of the Law

  And it came to pass, when Moses had made an end of writing the words of this law in a book, until they were finished. (Deuteronomy 31:24)

- Solomon finished the temple

  Thus Solomon finished the house of the LORD, *and the king's house: and all that came into Solomon's heart to make in the house of the* LORD, *and in his own house, he prosperously effected.* (2 Chronicles 7:11)

- Nehemiah finished the wall

  So the wall was finished in the twenty and fifth day of the month Elul, in fifty and two days. (Nehemiah 6:15)

- Ezra finished the second temple

  And this house was finished on the third day of the month Adar, which was in the sixth year of the reign of Darius the king. (Ezra 6:15)

- Jesus finished His work of salvation

  When Jesus therefore had received the vinegar, he said, It is finished: and he bowed his head, and gave up the ghost. (John 19:30)

Chapter 8 • Plan of Action and Time Management

- Paul finished his race

    I have fought a good fight, I have finished my course, I have kept the faith. (2 Timothy 4:7)

The Prophet Habakkuk said that even though your dreams or visions tarry, you are not to get impatient. Wait for them. In the end, they shall surely come to pass and will speak for themselves. (Habakkuk 2:2-3) Solomon, in his wisdom, uttered:

Better is the end of a thing than the beginning thereof: and the patient in spirit is better than the proud in spirit. (Ecclesiastes 7:8)

You see, God is not impressed with how great you begin but how great you finish. There are many great starters in the world but not many great finishers. The author of Hebrews declared, "…let us run with patience the race that is set before us" (Hebrews 12:1). It will definitely take commitment, tenacity and perseverance to see the fulfillment of your dream.

HAVE A PLAN OF ACTION

Now that you are committed to your dreams, it is imperative that you have a daily plan of actions that will get you there. You won't get there in one day. As the old song says, "One day at a time, Sweet Jesus..." will get you to them. What you do, daily, will produce powerful results.

Steady plodding brings prosperity; hasty speculation brings poverty. (Proverbs 21:5 TLB)

For a dream cometh through the multitude of business; and a fool's voice is known by multitude of words. (Ecclesiastes 5:3)

Your dreams will turn into realities as you work, steadily and aggressively, towards them. Dreams, destinies and goals do not just happen. You have got to get into some actions. James told us that faith without works is dead. We know the word "works" means "corresponding actions" and "faith" would be likened to the "dream" or "destiny".

Just as faith, without corresponding actions, is dead so is a dream without corresponding actions. Lazy people will not achieve anything. Achievers are dreamers and doers. Dreams without actions are mere wishes. Actions without dreams are wasted energies but dreams coupled with actions become realities.

Your actions must be complimentary to your dream. As simple as this sounds, it is one of the most overlooked principles. It is ludicrous to think that your dreams will be fulfilled when your actions are totally antagonistic towards them. Yet, that is how many people live their lives.

Imagine a man says he wants to be the heavyweight champion of the world but spends his time eating ice cream and smoking, without ever darkening the door of a gym. Do you think that this man has a chance to be the heavyweight champion of the world? No way! Not a chance! The only thing he can ever be is a heavy weight. As absurd as this sounds, it is a particular habit of so many believers who have lulled themselves into thinking that they can laze around, do stupid things and still fulfill their God given destiny. It will not happen.

After having a dream and setting up your goals, it becomes important to be diligent in pursuing your destiny. It is vital to have the right concept of diligent work, time management and excellence. These three will combine as powerful forces to your destiny. Let us scrutinize these three points more closely.

HARD WORK AND DILIGENCE

Though simplistic, one of the greatest keys to success is "an honest day's work." As a person of destiny, it is crucial that you tap into the law of work. I have taught my children about this law. I have explained this law to them in order for them to become "A" students. This law is universal – it will work for anyone who taps into it. The law of work states, "Work when you have to work and play when it is time to play. Do not mix the two". This is how you become a straight "A" student. It is not that the "C" student does not have the capacity; it's because they are easily distracted. They play when they should be working. Some people are in school but not in class. They might have been physically in class but their mind was all over the place.

I told my son, Ethan, "Son, when you are in class, make sure you focus on what the teacher is saying. This is not the time to play with your friends. When it is lunch time or break time, you can play as hard as you want. You can do cartwheels, jump, run and have all the fun you want to. But, in class, you work." This simple little rule will keep you in good standing throughout your life.

Just as we have discovered the ten characteristics of the lazy, the Bible also describes characteristics of the diligent. You see, many of us might deem ourselves to be diligent but does our idea of diligence compare to what the Scriptures say diligence is?

TEN CHARACTERISTICS OF THE DILIGENT

The word "diligent" in Hebrew is *charuwts*. It means "incised, incisive, threshing sledge, determination, eager, decision and to point sharply." It is from the Latin word *diligere* which means "to love, respect and take delight in". The dictionary defines diligent as "industrious, hard-working, particular, meticulous, painstaking, rigorous, careful, thorough, persevering, persistent, tenacious, zealous, dedicated, committed, unflagging, untiring, tireless and indefatigable". The Latin word is *diligo*, meaning "to love earnestly out of choice". To be diligent, therefore, implies deliberately loving what you do. To be diligent simply means to be constant in your efforts to accomplish what is undertaken. I would simply define "diligent" as having the ability to self-start and to be self-motivated. Let us peruse ten characteristics of the diligent:

1. The diligent works hard.

   He becometh poor that dealeth with a slack hand: but the hand of the diligent maketh rich. (Proverbs 10:4)

   Lazy people are soon poor; hard workers get rich. (Proverbs 10:4 NLT)

   > Doing your due diligence will bring you to your due season.

2. The diligent thinks and plans.

   The thoughts of the diligent tend only to plenteousness; but of every one that is hasty only to want. (Proverbs 21:5)

   Good planning and hard work lead to prosperity, but hasty shortcuts lead to poverty. (Proverbs 21:5 NLT)

3. The diligent is self motivated, uses his initiative, is disciplined and has stickability.

   Seest thou a man diligent in his business? he shall stand before kings; he shall not stand before mean men. (Proverbs 22:29)

   Do you see any truly competent workers? They will serve kings rather than working for ordinary people. (Proverbs 22:29 NLT)

4. The diligent is frugal.

   He also that is slothful in his work is brother to him that is a great waster. (Proverbs 18:9)

   The slothful man roasteth not that which he took in hunting: but the substance of a diligent man is precious. (Proverbs 12:27)

5. The diligent works wholeheartedly.

   And whatsoever ye do, do it heartily, as to the Lord, and not unto men; (Colossians 3:23)

Chapter 8 ● Plan of Action and Time Management

Whatsoever thy hand findeth to do, do it with thy might; for there is no work, nor device, nor knowledge, nor wisdom, in the grave, whither thou goest. (Ecclesiastes 9:10)

6. The diligent works on his mindset as much as he works with his hands.

    The thoughts of the diligent tend only to plenteousness; but of every one that is hasty only to want. (Proverbs 21:5)

7. The diligent is very thorough and precise, giving much attention to details.

    I call to remembrance my song in the night: I commune with mine own heart: and my spirit made diligent search. (Psalm 77:6)

8. The diligent is an early riser in contrast to the sluggard who loves sleep too much.

    And in the morning, rising up a great while before day, he went out, and departed into a solitary place, and there prayed. (Mark 1:35)

    Love not sleep, lest thou come to poverty; open thine eyes, and thou shalt be satisfied with bread. (Proverbs 20:13)

9. The diligent is proactive as opposed to the sluggard who procrastinates.

    He becometh poor that dealeth with a slack hand: but the hand of the diligent maketh rich. (Proverbs 10:4)

10. The diligent is time conscious, values time and will not waste time.

TIME MANAGEMENT

Time management skills are essential for success. Those who have the knack to successfully implement time management strategies will be rightly positioned to effectively control their destiny. That's in contrast to stressfully spending their day in a frenzy of activities, going from crisis to crisis, thus reducing their productivity ratio. The time management skilled person is highly proactive. They focus on the tasks that will have the greatest impact on their dream.

What is time management? Time management is simply deciding what the right priority is and doing it. This sounds simple but most people do not get this right. Some people's lives are so frantic because they have not figured out what priority is. The consequences of poor time management are defined by the following:

- Procrastination
- Last minute rushes to meet deadlines
- Unproductive days
- Stress
- Missing deadlines
- Distractions
- Inability to perform due to lack of preparation
- Poor quality work

TIME IS THE CURRENCY OF EXCHANGE

To eliminate the above, you must grasp the concept of time management. Here are some clues that indicate that you have not yet mastered time management.

- You wished there was more time in the day
- You are habitually late
- You have no set time to wake up or go to sleep
- You do not operate from a planner or diary
- You double book appointments or miss important appointments

- You do not pay your bills on time therefore incurring extra fees
- You feel overwhelmed by the tasks you have to achieve
- You try to multitask
- You do not set time increments to projects
- You are easily distracted by television, telephones, social media and people

TIME IS YOUR BIGGEST ASSET

Procrastination, disorganization, and interruptions are time thieves. Time management is an art or skill that you will have to learn. The first thing you have to learn is that time is the biggest asset God has given you. We all have 24 hours a day. It is what you do in those 24 hours that will determine your destiny and future. Being skillful with your 24 hour increments will be the key to success. The average person sleeps 8 hours daily, works 8 hours and has the remaining 8 hours for himself. Unfortunately, most spend these hours as a couch potato, watching television when they could learn a new skill or update their information bank by reading a book or completing a course.

Whatever you give time to is what you will have in life. Whatever you do not give time to is what you can never possess. Anything you want in life will be determined by the amount of time you give to it. Wishing that you can play the guitar is not going to become a reality if you do not give time to it. Wishing that you are a great basketball player will not materialize if you do not spend time practicing.

Time is the currency of exchange. Money is transacted, per hour, as wages. The more skillful one is in a field – due to the time he invested to make himself an expert – the more he gets remunerated per hour. An expert is simply someone who invested a lot of time in a particular field. This is why you must strive to be in the top 10 percent of your field. It is the expert who commands great finances. If you want to be in the top 10 percent of income earners, then invest time and be a high level learner. Here are some thoughts on time management to help you be more efficient:

1. Wake up early.

The very first thing you will have to understand about time management is the need to be disciplined. Time management will kill wayward living. One of the ways you can add more time to your day is simply by waking up early. If you have been saying, "I just wish there was more time in the day". Then, there is! Not that you can make a day become 25 hours. It simply means that by waking up earlier, you get to maximize more of the 24 hour day. The old adage that says, "The early bird gets the worm" is true for the bird and you. Waking up early gives you time to prepare for your day. It gives you additional hours to do specific things such as reading the Scriptures, praying or exercising. Morning work outs are best.

I cannot stress, enough, the importance of going to bed at the right time. Getting sufficient rest and waking up fresh is paramount to a successful day. Being tired does not leave you at your best. The tendency to laze around or fall asleep when you should be working is not good time management. The Scripture says, "It is vain to go to bed late and to wake up early." Early to bed and early to rise should be your motto. Now, I am not saying for you to go to bed at 8:00 PM. However, go to sleep at a reasonable hour. Go to bed before midnight and wake up early. I have had to train myself to do this.

For years, I prided myself in the fact that I went to bed in the early hours of the morning and woke up around 7:00 AM. I thought I was being productive. But, most of the time, I was tired and irritated

Chapter 8 ● Plan of Action and Time Management

during the day. I would drink a lot of coffee to stay awake. Now, I have retrained myself to go to bed before midnight and wake up between 5:00 and 6:00 AM. I get more accomplished this way. Most of my business communications is overseas. So, being awake at 5:00 AM is great because of the time zones in different nations.

2. Learn to operate from a daily planner.

Plan your day the night before you go to sleep or early in the morning. Do your best to stick to that schedule. This is one of the most important aspects of time management.

Your daily planner is setting your daily goals which will trigger daily satisfaction and daily success. Your daily planner sets the order of the day. It reveals what is important and what is minor. It gives you a point of reference. Whether you use a diary, an e-planner app, an iPad or laptop, it simply records some things which are to be achieved for the day. In this way, you are not relying on your mind. If it is not recorded, the likelihood of forgetting it is very high. Whether you write it down or type it into your e-planner, the fact that you recorded it helps to stop people from distracting you. Train yourself to operate from a planner. You might fail at it a few times. Nevertheless, keep doing it until it becomes part of your daily routine.

My school principal, Rev. Lindsey Mann, taught me about the power of a diary, daily planning and the power of your word. I will be forever grateful and indebted to him for such simple but very powerful principles. The act of learning to plan a day will help you plan a year and your life. Keep to your schedule and keep to your word. If you are not true to yourself you won't be true to others.

3. Give increments of time to a specific project without distraction.

Whatever you are tackling needs to be given ample time for preparation and execution to obtain the desired result. When I first went into full time ministry I had no meetings and administration to speak of. However, I would faithfully be in the Word from 9:00 AM till 1:00 PM and be in prayer from 2:00 - 4:00 PM. These days, although I am very busy, I still live by the same rule of giving increments of time to a particular task.

I spend most of my time on airplanes; some of the flights can be 12 hours long. What am I going to do with those twelve hours? A lot of people just eat, drink, watch movies and sleep. I will give increments of time to reading or writing books.

When I am writing a book, I will say, "By such and such time, I will begin and finish." Or, I can say, "Today I will write two chapters of this particular book." I go into my Holy Room, where nothing happens except for prayer. I put on some soft music – usually instrumentals that are soothing and cause me to think about what I am writing.

This particular chapter of the book you are reading was written on a flight from Amsterdam to Detroit. I knew the flight would be over 8 hours; therefore, I planned how many hours I would utilize to write. There are no phone calls on flights. So, since I do not know anyone on this plane, there are no distractions. Learn to give an increment of two hours to a specific task, daily, and you will make great strides.

4. Protect your day and focus without silly distractions.

You do not have to answer every call that comes in. Pick and choose who you will speak to. When the phone rings, they may want to speak to you but it is at your discretion whether to answer or not. Some people just love to talk on the phone when they have nothing to do. This is the purpose of voicemail. If it is really important, the caller will leave a voicemail message. Just because someone does not have anything to do does not mean that you do not have things on

Chapter 8 • Plan of Action and Time Management

your plate. Screen your calls. If you have to answer the call during business hours, minimize the call to the business of the call without reminiscing over old stories. There is a time for that but not within working hours. Do not feel guilty over not answering a call from a friend. When you do not answer a friend's call that does not make you their enemy. It simply means that you are busy, at the time, attending to important issues.

5. Set a time to make your phone calls and answer emails.

With the constant bombardment of Facebook, Twitter and other aspects of social media, it is very easy to get caught up with these activities and be taken away from what is important. If you have to do Twitter and Facebook then use an app that covers multiple apps. Some apps can be timed to send out updates at certain times of the day. Make the phone calls that you have to make, without procrastinating. Overcome the fear of calling and talking to unknown people. I usually look at my planner to determine when I will make calls or send emails. I do them whether I feel like it or not. They are part of my duties and responsibilities. I usually write the names of the people in my planner. Once I have called them, I check off their name. If I called but did not get an answer, I still put a tick by their name and then cross the tick to indicate that I did not get them. Create a system which works for you.

6. Plan your priority time and your pleasure time.

You have to schedule the moments of your life. You have to create memorable times. Growing up in London, life was very hectic for the family. Everyone was going in their respective directions. We scheduled Sunday evenings, after church service, as special family time. We had a great meal, together as a family. We would all be sitting around the table and joking with one another and friends that came over.

As focused as you are, you also need some time just for yourself. This is time to do things that you enjoy. Maybe it is going to the gym or walking. You have to schedule that time in your planner. Otherwise, it will not happen. Also, schedule family time and fun time.

7. Don't try to multitask.

For a while, there was a great emphasis on multitasking. You heard people say, "I'm going to kill two birds with one stone." Give your attention and time to a single task and do it well. It's better to do one thing with excellence than to do many things in mediocre ways. Multitasking is simply an indication that you have not learned the power and benefits of delegation. Do not be afraid to delegate and ask people to help you. If you can afford to, hire skillful people to get the results you need. I am not good at everything, I am good at certain things and I give a hundred percent to them.

8. Improve your skills.

Improving your skills and abilities will get you the desired results quicker. Knowing how to operate a computer will give you quicker results than not knowing how to run a computer. Whatever skill you develop will determine what you can achieve quicker than others. Honing your skills is a great way to get results in less time. It frees you to achieve other things. Having skills gives you confidence to obtain the right results. What can take some people an hour to do can take a skillful person ten minutes to do.

9. Keep up with modern technology.

The purpose of technology is to make things faster and more efficient. Remember when there was no fax or email and letters were the primary form of communication? Going to the Post Office, buying a stamp and mailing a letter that will take a week to get overseas is now replaced by sending an instant email. Now, that is efficient time management.

Chapter 8 • Plan of Action and Time Management

Today, through the internet, I can be in Nigeria and talk to my wife and kids on Skype in America. As a matter of fact, I can leave Skype on all day long and it is like I am home without being home. Being an itinerant minister or missionary is not what it used to be centuries ago. Years ago, missionaries would go to distant lands and their families would not hear from them for months at a time. Now, through modern technology, your family is at your fingertips. If a machine can do it then let the machine do it; you get on to doing something else.

Machines and computers are not emotional. They will simply do what they are told to do. The purpose of technology is to give you better results in a shorter amount of time than previous generations. Therefore, take advantage of them. I am always looking for whatever can give me quicker results.

Some people just refuse to change their antiquated ways. If I can get my email, voicemail, internet, Skype, texts, GPS, Siri, Bank Apps, online payments, and more on my phone, then why waste time using the old technology? Nowadays, you can find an app for almost anything. My friend, it is time to update yourself before you quickly become a living relic of the former century.

> A dream without corresponding actions is dead.

Now, I have heard the old excuse, "But it's all daunting to me!" Here is the thing: gadgets come with instructions. There are also plenty of people willing to show you how they work. Ask for help. Now, you can google anything and get the help you need. These are great days to be alive and to achieve great things quicker. Let us not live as 19th and 20th century people. You are alive in the 21st century. Take advantage of the technology available to you. Invest in technology. That is one of the smartest time management skills you can ever acquire.

10. Invest in new equipment and never stop learning.

Remember, today's excellence is tomorrow's mediocrity. Every few months, they are coming out with new software, apps, and machines that will decrease the time needed to obtain results. What was efficient two years ago may be obsolete next year. So, always be on the lookout to invest in better equipment. Buy new apps! Buy new software! Buy a new machine or a better laptop that gives you everything at your fingertips. Do not be looking for hand-me-downs from your friends of their old machines. If it is not good enough for them, it is not good enough for you.

Always remain inquisitive and be an avid learner. Develop a voracious appetite for information that keeps you on the cutting edge of life, business or ministry. Learning will give you speed to catch up with those ahead of you. They may have become satisfied. So, you can overtake those who are refusing to upgrade their learning capacity.

There are many books and materials available to help you in time management. Invest in them. Many times, investing $100 or even $500, to learn about a specific field, will bring thousands of dollars back to you. Never think that the investment is too much. It is never too much to invest in yourself. The returns are outstanding.

11. Establish a filing system.

Keep your records, receipts and other paper work filed, alphabetically. Be able to quickly retrieve them when you need them. So much time is wasted looking for paperwork that was not properly filed or stored. I have learned this the hard way. As already mentioned, you will need to be disciplined in order to manage time. Therefore, it is imperative that you have order in your life. Do not waste time looking for keys, contracts and important papers.

Chapter 8 ● Plan of Action and Time Management

God is a God of order. Everything is in its proper place. Look at your body! Everything is in its proper place. God did not put your nose on your toe as you would inhale dust. He did not put your eyes on the side of your head where your ears are. You would only be able to see what is on your side and not what is in front of you. Order is defined as "a state in which everything is in its correct or appropriate place".

What do you do when you get home from work? Do you throw your keys, shoes and clothes all over the house or do you put them in a place where you will be able to quickly retrieve them? You must become orderly. Are your pockets full of receipts and your table full of paper work and mail? That indicates that you are administratively challenged. And, it will be a problem in the long run. Get organized now! The disorganized can get away with some stuff; eventually, he will be found out. It pays to be organized. It does not mean that you are obsessive or controlling. It is wisdom!

PART III

THE SATISFACTION TO SAY, "SWEET"

DEVELOPING MILLION DOLLAR HABITS

Chapter 9

In pursuing your goals and destiny, you will definitely need to develop key character traits that will enable your transition from obscurity to influence. Some people call these crucial components "million dollar habits". Allow me to give you what I deem as the six most important million dollar habits:

> It takes consistent, high-level performance to achieve greatness.

A NEVER QUIT ATTITUDE

Do not falter when tough times challenge your dreams. This one thing is for sure: your dreams will be challenged by satan, people, situations and even your loved ones. Remember, Joseph and his brothers in Genesis 37? Every great achiever was challenged and you are no exception. You have to make up your mind never to quit. Quitting is a habit of destruction.

Crisis is a part of life for a dreamer. Get used to it! The storms of life come to everybody. You are not immune from them. But, you can overcome them. Taking the path of least resistance is the runway to failure. The Apostle Paul told us to fight the good fight of faith (1 Tim. 6:12). Fight to make your dreams come true. What satan throws at you as challenges to your dreams, use as stepping stones to launch you into the blessings of God.

Remember, if you do not run from the challenges and storms, then, they will run from you. Challenges reveal that you are moving toward promotion. People who take the path of least resistance will never soar in life. Yes, your dreams will be sorely challenged. However, if you refuse to quit, you will eventually soar. Those who refuse to quit will soar in life.

I heard a true story of a man who found an emperor moth cocoon. He wanted to watch the moth breaking out of the cocoon, so he took the cocoon to his house. The day came when it looked like the moth was going to make his way out of the small opening. The man sat and watched, for several hours, as the moth struggled to force its body through that little hole. The moth was struggling for quite some time. It looked stuck and appeared to have stopped making progress. It seemed as if the moth had gone as far as it could and could go no further.

The man decided to help the moth. So, he took a pair of scissors and cut off the remaining bit of the cocoon. This helped the moth to easily come forth. Soon, the moth emerged, but it had a swollen body and small, shriveled wings. The man continued to watch the moth, expecting it to grow and fly. It did not happen! In fact, the little moth spent the rest of its life crawling around with a small, swollen body and shriveled wings. It never was able to fly. Though kind, the man did not understand that the struggle was imperative for the moth to get through the tiny opening. The struggle would have forced fluid from its body onto its wings so that it would be ready for flight. Freedom and flight would only come after the struggle. By supposedly helping the moth out of a struggle, he deprived the moth of health.

Struggles are part of turning your dreams into reality. Though we do not appreciate pain when we are experiencing it, pain causes us to have strong wings to soar in life. By struggles, I am not referring

Chapter 9 • Developing Million Dollar Habits

to sickness and disease. Jesus already redeemed us from those. I am talking about opposition and obstacles to your destiny. Just like the moth or butterfly, if we were to go through life without any opposition, we would be crippled. We would not be as strong as we could have been. Do not quit! You will discover, in the middle of your struggle, that you are growing wings to soar high in life.

CHOOSE RIGHT ASSOCIATIONS

Association with the right kinds of people is paramount to your success. It is a million dollar habit to develop the right relationships. Who you associate with, will either defile you or deploy you. Many are stuck in detrimental relationships, out of habit. They do not know how to break free of them. Some are in these relationships because of emotional ties. Many are loyal to those who are destructive to their future. Yet, to them, it seems illogical to walk away from these associations.

> Your associations will determine your assimilation and impartation.

> *He that walketh with wise men shall be wise: but a companion of fools shall be destroyed.* (Proverbs 13:20)

Your associations will determine your assimilation and impartation. Simply put, we become like those we spend time with – good or bad.

> *There is desirable treasure, And oil in the dwelling of the wise, But a foolish man squanders it.* (Proverbs 21:20 NKJV)

Young's Literal Translation says it this way, "A treasure to be desired, and oil, is in the habitation of the wise, and a foolish man swalloweth it up."

Success breeds success and failures breed failures. Your associations will make or break you. From today on, evaluate those who are in relationship with you. What are the dynamics? There is no such thing as a neutral relationship.

- **Relationships are spiritual**. They are either taking you closer to God or removing you from God.
- **Relationships are mental**. They will either give you peace of mind or a mental breakdown.
- **Relationships are professional**. They will either take you to your destiny or away from it.
- **Relationships are consequential.** The consequence of the association will either be negative or positive.

As you journey to your destiny, it is your responsibility to foster "destiny" relationships and forsake "detrimental" relationships. Do not think that you can handle a bad relationship and not suffer the consequences. If you flirt with that which is forbidden, do not be surprised when you fall into its trap. Do not give your time to people who do not value your dreams. People who do not increase you will eventually decrease you.

Find people who have done what you want to do, stay around them and learn. Do not fellowship with nor expose your dreams to non-dreamers. You cannot get to the palace by hanging around peasants. There are people around you – and they may be close relatives – who have peasant mentalities. They enjoy running you down and laughing at your expense. Run from them as you would from a rattlesnake. Fellowship with people of faith who will encourage and uplift you. If you are getting blessed, then hang around the blessed. Here are some powerful thoughts on associations:

- Your association determines whether you taste victory or defeat
- Your association is either taking you into or removing you from your chosen destiny
- Your association unveils the condition of your heart
- Your association is a prediction of your future

- Your association determines whether you are influenced for better or for worse
- Your association determines your assimilation

Surround yourself with people who are motivated. Associate with people who are more talented than you are. Do not be threatened by more skillful or educated people than yourself. Thrive on their skills and knowledge. To be the best, you have to learn from the best. The people you call friends will make you who you are.

BE A PERSON OF YOUR WORD

> *When you vow a vow to God, do not delay paying it, for he has no pleasure in fools. Pay what you vow. It is better that you should not vow than that you should vow and not pay. Let not your mouth lead you into sin, and do not say before the messenger that it was a mistake. Why should God be angry at your voice and destroy the work of your hands?* (Ecclesiastes 5:4-6 ESV)

If your word is no good then you are no good. This is a habit that I cannot stress enough. You and your word must be one. Establish a reputation for being a man of your word. It does not matter if it costs you something in the short run; it will pay you in the long run. The moment people discover that you do not keep your word, your destiny will be in decline. Let your "yes" be "yes" and your "no" be "no".

Have you ever noticed how many people do not keep their word? It could be as small as not calling when they said they would or as large as the vow "till death do us part". To so many people, including believers and ministers, their word means nothing. People do not realize that if their word is nothing then they are nothing!

> Life is full of people who over promise and under perform.

Life is full of people who over promise and under perform. It is stupefying how many people do not follow through on their word. Your ability to be a man of your word will be the bedrock and foundation of your brand and identification. Often overlooked but needing to be remembered is this: Not keeping your word is equal to being a liar. Therefore, be minimal in what you promise but over perform when you do give it.

Do your utmost to keep your word. If for some reason you cannot keep your word, you are better off calling to honestly apologize beforehand. Remember, no one is perfect and stuff happens beyond your control. So, don't beat yourself up about it. You have to have the reputation that you are a person of integrity and that your word is good. If you promise to do something, then do it. Stop making excuses! You are only hurting yourself.

Ecclesiastes 7:1 says, "A good name is better than precious ointment..."

1. Keep your word to God.
2. Keep your word to yourself.
3. Keep your word to your spouse.
4. Keep your word to your family.
5. Keep your word to your employer.
6. Keep your word to your friends.

Keeping your word enhances your reputation. And, it is a sure way to enable success in your destiny.

BE PUNCTUAL

Some people think it is fashionable to be habitually late. For some, the notion of being on time is nearly impossible. Trust is broken when you are always late. You become a time thief when you are always late. In other words, you are robbing people of their time and putting them in a place of frustration and anger. Being late creates an image of being disorganized. It is a very bad first impression that becomes difficult to shake. Being punctual is a million dollar habit that you need to master. God deems punctuality as important. The Bible talks about the "appointed time" or the "fullness of time". See what Paul said to the Galatians:

> But when the fullness of the time had come, God sent forth His Son, born of a woman, born under the law. (Galatians 4:4)

I especially love the Living Bible translation of this verse, "But when the right time came, the time God decided on, he sent his Son." We may not see punctuality as important, but God does! I want to look at the pros of punctuality and the cons of tardiness.

> *I have generally found that the man who is good at an excuse is good for nothing else.* –Benjamin Franklin speaking to an often late employee

Pros of punctuality
- Punctuality unveils integrity and credibility
- Punctuality unveils trustworthiness and dependability
- Punctuality unveils and breeds discipline
- Punctuality unveils respect for others
- Punctuality unveils competence
- Punctuality relieves tension, stress and embarrassment

Cons of lateness
- Lateness frustrates relationships
- Lateness invites stress and embarrassment
- Lateness shows disrespect
- Lateness causes missed opportunity
- Lateness wastes the precious time of others
- Lateness makes you a time thief

BE DRIVEN AND HAVE A STRONG WORK ETHIC

Hard work as a key to success is a well-known adage. Parents and teachers drive children to work hard so that they can get good grades and have better options or a better career. One thing you will notice about those who have their dreams fulfilled is that they work hard. They are very diligent. In the Bible, other terms for lazy people are slothful, sluggard and slack. Lazy people are wasters. They waste time, energy and life. They are always full of excuses. They always procrastinate.

If you recognize these traits in yourself, you need to eradicate them. Learn to be diligent. Never be afraid to put your back into it. Any person who will excel in his life and career will do so through the diligence of hard work. Here are two great quotes to meditate upon:

> *Without ambition, one starts nothing. Without work, one finishes nothing. The prize will not be sent to you. You have to win it.*
> – Ralph Waldo Emerson

> *We often miss opportunity because it's dressed in overalls and looks like work.* –Thomas Edison

I want you to understand that talent does not necessarily mean intelligence, drive and motivation. Talent on its own will not guarantee success. Diligence and hard work must be attached to it.

> The proof of excellence is distinction and prominence.

It is naive to think that if you find the field where you are naturally gifted, it will spur you to greatness. It takes consistent, high-level performance to achieve greatness. It requires you to maintain a drive for hard work. What do we mean by hard work?

- Consistently work on improving or honing your skills
- Never think you have arrived
- Check out the competition and see what they are doing that you are not

Chapter 9 • Developing Million Dollar Habits

- Cultivate the character of excellence and become a finisher
- Comply with time making time work for and not against you
- Commit to be productive, daily
- Cut off wrong people
- Eliminate procrastination
- Eradicate a lackluster attitude

WORK SMART

In addition to being diligent and working hard, you have to learn to work smart. This is a great key to seeing quicker results in your life, ministry and career. Learn to work hard at working smart. To work smart does not mean that you cut corners and compromise. Work more intelligently as opposed to harder. Choose the most efficient use of your time and energy before you act. It simply means, you tap into what triggers fast, desired results. How do you do that?

Pose questions. Is what I am doing the best way to get the results I desire? Ask questions of yourself and the people around you. Ask a professional or someone who has done what you want to do.

Plan and prioritize. Without planning and prioritizing, you will be all over the place. God is a master planner. Learn to plan your life. Plan a day, a week and a year. Then, have a five-year plan. Make it your priority to know what the priorities in your life and business are.

Protect Productive, Personal Relationships. Protect the right relationships and walk away from relationships that are not a priority. The right person will deploy your life and the wrong person will defile your life. Cultivate a close and personal relationship with those whose gift and talent can deploy your greatness. The right person in your life is a door that will save you years of trying to make it happen by yourself.

Combining a strong work ethic and working smart will be catalysts for great change in your life. I live my life by this simple little instruction, "Be relentless in the pursuit of your dream and ruthless with distractions and detractors." That principle has kept me in good standing throughout my life.

> Be relentless in the pursuit of your dream and ruthless with distractions and detractors.

STRIVE FOR EXCELLENCE

Whatever you do, do it with excellence. As you pursue your destiny, you have to establish a reputation for being a person of excellence. Here is a verse that you need to measure your life by:

> *Seest thou a man diligent in his business? he shall stand before kings; he shall not stand before mean men.* (Proverbs 22:29)

Notice the word, "diligent". In Hebrew, it is the word, *mahiyr* meaning skillful, quick, diligent, flow, competent and excel. A modern rendition of this verse would be, "Do you see a man who is quick, diligent, skillful, competent and excellent in his business? This will bring him before great men." That is how you should judge your life. You see, many are legends in their own minds – thinking that they are excellent. Your excellence is proven by your coming before great men. Sooner or later, your level of excellence will give you a presence and bring you to prominence. This is echoed by the wisdom of Proverbs:

> *A man's gift maketh room for him, and bringeth him before great men.* (Proverbs 18:16)

So what do we mean by excellence?

DEFINING EXCELLENCE

Excellence comes from the ancient Greek word *arete*. In its basic sense, it means excellence of any kind. However the word *arete* was

Chapter 9 • Developing Million Dollar Habits

ultimately bound with the notion of the fulfillment of purpose. It came to refer to living up to one's full potential. From the word *arete* we got the word *aristos* – from which we get the word "aristocrat" and "aristocracy" which mean nobility. Therefore, excellence is the art of distinction in your chosen field that comes by being meticulously attentive to details. When you look back over your life, it will be the little details that you neglected that will cause you big problems.

> *Take us the foxes, the little foxes, that spoil the vines: for our vines have tender grapes.* (Song of Solomon 2:15)

Excellence, therefore, is giving your best on a daily basis. It is always looking for a way to improve and progress without resting on yesterday's accomplishment. Brian Tracy's definition is "excellence/perfection is not a destination; it is a continuous journey that never ends." What is excellent today will not be excellent tomorrow. We see this in technology. The latest thing today will become obsolete, in time. We grew up playing records, then audio tapes, which were later replaced by CDs, then mp3s. Technology keeps improving and progressing. That is excellence!

The dictionary defines "excellence" as the quality of being outstanding. The nemesis of excellence is mediocrity – a combination of two Latin words, *medius* meaning "middle" and *ocris* referring to a mountain. Hence, mediocrity simply means halfway up the mountain. It is not mountain peak performance; it is being average. Do not ever settle for being average. Strive to be the best. Strive to be excellent. Daniel had a reputation for having a spirit of excellence.

> *Forasmuch as an excellent spirit, and knowledge, and understanding, interpreting of dreams, and shewing of hard sentences, and dissolving of doubts, were found in the same Daniel, whom the king named Belteshazzar: now let Daniel be called, and he will shew the interpretation.*
> (Daniel 5:12)

> *Then this Daniel was preferred above the presidents and princes, because an excellent spirit was in him; and the king thought to set him over the whole realm.* (Daniel 6:3)

> *Daniel soon proved himself more capable than all the other administrators and high officers. Because of Daniel's great ability, the king made plans to place him over the entire empire.* (Daniel 6:3 NLT)

The proof of excellence is distinction. Daniel served in the administrations of Nebuchadnezzar, Belteshazzar, Darius and Cyrus. The older he got, the more indispensable he became. Why? Because, he had a spirit of excellence. Notice that he was summoned by the administrations because he was distinguished and excellent.

Excellence will keep you relevant, all the days of your life. Excellence keeps you indispensable. So many, as they get older, are viewed as over the hill, ineffective and replaceable. Not so in the case of Daniel. The older he became the more valuable he became! This is why you must strive to be distinguished so that even in your old age, you are still wanted and the competition cannot take you out. If the proof of desire is pursuit and the proof of pursuit is progress then the proof of excellence is distinction. What habits can you incorporate to remain relevant throughout the years? I conclude this chapter on million dollar habits with these:

- The constant pursuit of improvement
- The constant development of your skills
- The constant seeking of distinction

WISDOM FROM AGUR'S FOUR LITTLE CREATURES

Chapter 10

Proverbs, the book of wisdom, gives us great keys on how to live successfully in every facet of our lives. Although most of Proverbs is attributed to Solomon, there were other respective authors:

- The Sayings of the Wise
- The Words of Agur
- King Lemuel of Massa

In this chapter, we will look at a small portion of the wisdom of Agur.

> Little is big when wisdom is applied.

> *The words of Agur the son of Jakeh, even the prophecy... There be four things which are little upon the earth, but they are exceeding wise: The ants are a people not strong, yet they prepare their meat in the summer; The conies are but a feeble folk, yet make they their houses in the rocks; The locusts have no king, yet go they forth all of them by bands; The spider taketh hold with her hands, and is in kings" palaces.* (Proverbs 30:1, 24-28)

Not much is known about Agur. From his name, we understand certain things. *Agur* means "gatherer". Therefore, we can conclude that he was a gatherer of wisdom after having observed the four little creatures in the Middle East. He, then, imparts great wisdom to those who will take heed on how to live successfully in life. The wisdom of Agur will hopefully encourage and motivate you in the right direction.

SMALL THINGS

Agur said, "There are four things on earth that are small but unusually wise." The first point I want to make is that great things can come in small packages. Secondly, little is big when wisdom is applied. Thirdly, size does not matter. What look like disadvantages can be turned to your advantages. Never underestimate small things. In fact, we are told, neglect not the days of small beginnings.

God used an ant, a coney, a locust and a spider to give us wisdom. To most people, the ant and the three respective creatures would have been overlooked and never been the subject of any lesson. When we think of magnificent creatures, an ant does not come to mind. Most westerners do not have a clue as to what a coney is. When we think of great animals, our minds would revert to the lion, the horse or the elephant. I have visited South Africa, many times. There, they talk about the Big Five: the buffalo, elephant, leopard, rhino and lion. It would seem that God would have used these magnificent five to teach us wisdom for life, management and business. Yet, God overlooked the Big Five and went after the small four. Agur told us there is exceeding wisdom in these tiny four little creatures:

LESSONS FROM THE ANT

Agur states, "The ants are a people not strong, yet they prepare their meat in the summer." In all of Scripture, the ant is mentioned twice. Here are the two references for the ant.

> *Go to the ant, thou sluggard; consider her ways, and be wise: Which having no guide, overseer, or ruler, Provideth her meat in the summer, and gathereth her food in the harvest. How long wilt thou sleep, O sluggard? when wilt thou arise out of thy sleep? Yet a little sleep, a little slumber, a little folding of the hands to sleep: So shall thy poverty come as one that travelleth, and thy want as an armed man.* (Proverbs 6:6-11)

Chapter 10 ● Wisdom from Agur's Four Little Creatures

> *The ants are a people not strong, yet they prepare their meat in the summer.* (Proverbs 30:25)

So, what can we learn from the ant? I want to give you ten important lessons from this tiny creature.

1. The ant teaches us that wisdom is better than physical strength.

"The ants are a people not strong..." Spiritual and mental strength is the key to prosperity. Wisdom exceeds physical limitations. Those who make their living by their strength will eventually be limited. But, those who make their living by their minds will always have the edge over the physically strong.

2. The ant teaches us to understand the seasons of life and how to position and prepare for the seasons.

As a matter of fact, the ant prepares for the winter in the summer. He does not think that summer will last forever. He uses the summer to work in order to be satisfied in the winter. Living in Kentucky, where we experience the four seasons, I have noticed the ants are very visible in the summer; but, I do not see them in the winter. Do you know what I have seen in the winter, trying to get into my house? The mouse, looking for warmth and food. Why? Because the mouse was busy living it up in the summer and looking cool. The ant, on the other hand, was busy working.

3. The ant teaches us to be two seasons ahead.

He prepares for the winter in the summer. He does not prepare for the winter in the winter – or even in the fall. The ant is two seasons ahead. He has the mind to work in the summer time in order to rest in the winter time. When you are between the ages of 16-62, you are in the summer of your life. The world calls this period your earning years. While you can enjoy this season –and you should – you should have the vision to put stuff away for the winter season of your life. Always think ahead! Always be ahead of the game. Use time, now, to prepare for the future! The ant teaches us that you do not prepare for emergencies in times of emergencies but in the time of ease.

4. The ant teaches us to turn your disadvantages to your advantage and profit.

Your little finger is bigger than the ant. It is very small and insignificant. From all angles, when you look at it, there is nothing striking about the ant. Yet, he turns his obstacles into opportunities. Whatever you think your disadvantages are, you can turn them and make them work for you.

5. The ant teaches us that size does not matter and does not determine your potential.

Although small in stature, the ant fulfills his potential and feeds his family. It teaches us that it is not what you look like on the outside that determines how well you do in life but how big you are on the inside. The ant is small in physical stature but big in mental stature.

6. The ant teaches us to be industrious and hardworking.

The ant is not afraid of work. He is indefatigable and industrious. This is a great key to success in life. Those who are lazy invite poverty. The ant is the antithesis of poverty.

7. The ant teaches us to seize our opportunities when they come.

Opportunities will always come. Are you ready for them or do you not recognize them because they usually look like work? The ant saw the opportunity in the summer and seized it. The important point is that you must see the opportunity in order to seize it.

Chapter 10 • Wisdom from Agur's Four Little Creatures

8. The ant teaches us that preparations, planning, pro-actions and perseverance are the foresight and insight we need for life's eventualities.

Life's eventualities are certain. It does not matter who you are, there are some things which are inescapable. For example, no matter what you do to stem back the tide, you will still get old. Secondly, if the Lord Jesus tarries, you will die. There are no two ways about it. However, you do not have to be caught unaware. The ant teaches us that we must be aware of life's eventualities and be ready for them. You must look at life through the lenses of insight and foresight.

9. The ant teaches us that there is power to fulfill purpose as a team.

Agur stated, "The ants are a people not strong..." People implies plurality of persons. Have you ever seen a colony of ants moving a dead insect – way bigger and heavier than they – to their destination? They synchronize their energy and strength to move heavier weights than themselves. He knows that by himself he is limited; with a team, he can move his purpose forward. Are you a loner or do you have a team around you?

10. The ant teaches us that preparation brings provision and that poverty and lack are avoidable.

Lack of provision indicates lack of preparation. By preparation we mean setting things in their proper order. Poverty can be avoided. Poverty is not an indication of a lack of money. Poverty is an indication of misplaced, misused and misguided money. Lack is an indication that you never prepared your money to work for you. The ant prepares. How about you?

> The nugget from the ant: He prepares!

LESSONS FROM THE CONEY

What in the world is a coney? Modern translations of the Bible use the word, "rock badger" instead of "coney". People have tried to say that this is a rabbit. Conies look like rabbits, yet they are not rabbits. The rabbit is fast and can run. Conies' hind legs are its weakest point. So, they are not strong enough to run. The conies are small creatures very common in the Middle East. In today's world, they are known as the rock hyrax. Agur stated, "The conies are but a feeble folk, yet make they their houses in the rocks..." Hyraxes are preyed upon by leopards, pythons, large birds, big cats and civets. They protect themselves from smaller predators by biting. Escaping to hiding places among the rocks is their best defense. So, what can we learn from the coney or rock hyrax?

1. The coney teaches us that we have enemies.

Conies are called a "feeble folk" by Agur and that he has enemies who want to treat him as prey. Believe it or not, the coney is related to the elephant yet, he does not possess the strength nor the size of his colossal relative. Being small makes him a target for the eagle and other predators. Enemies to your welfare and betterment are real. The coney teaches us to be aware of our enemies.

2. The coney teaches us that we must know our limitations.

Although related to the elephant, the coney does not live within the protection of the elephant. Being small, he is limited. However, he is aware of his shortcomings. His hind legs are not strong nor do they give him the speed to outrun his enemies. He may look similar to a rabbit or a hare but he does not have the speed of these two. Hence, he does not expose himself, openly, to his predators. He hides within the rock.

Chapter 10 • Wisdom from Agur's Four Little Creatures

3. The coney teaches us that in order to stop being easy prey, we must locate the rock of defense.

The coney does not roam about in the wild. He stays within the safety of his house, the rock. Your safety is in the house built upon the rock of God's word. Roaming, aimlessly and wildly, in the jungle of life, will expose you to your enemies. Every believer must build his house upon the Rock.

4. The coney teaches us that our salvation and safety is in Christ the Rock.

Paul tells the Corinthians that the Rock is Christ. To be truly saved from your enemies, you have to be in Christ the Rock. If any man be in Christ, then he is a new creature and all things are passed away.

5. The coney teaches us to be vigilant.

When the conies are eating, they make a circle and stand with their faces looking outside the circle. This way, they can spot any intruder or predator. They do not just eat, face down, and oblivious to their enemies. Peter told us, "Be sober, be vigilant; because your adversary the devil, as a roaring lion, walketh about, seeking whom he may devour." To protect yourself and your family, you need to be vigilant.

6. The coney teaches us to stay in the Sun of Righteousness.

The conies spend a lot of time sun-bathing. About 95 percent of the time it is resting. This can involve heaping – in which they pile on top of each other inside a den – or basking in the sun. Both behaviors are compensations for the hyrax's poorly developed thermoregulation (the ability to regulate the body's temperature). As believers, who are endeavoring to be successful, we must keep ourselves before the Sun of Righteousness – The Lord Jesus – and remember it is He who gives us the power to get wealth.

7. The coney teaches us to maintain the joy of the Lord and keep our praise on.

Conies have at least 21 different vocalizations, including trills, yips, grunts, wails, snorts, twitters, shrieks, growls, and whistles. Males also sing complex songs that can last for several minutes and serve a territorial purpose, like a bird song. When researchers looked at how males put together different syllables (wails, chucks, snorts, squeaks, and tweets) to compose a song, they found the order of the syllables was significant. Hyrax songs make use of syntax, the manner in which different elements are combined. They also found hyraxes from different regions used different local dialects in their songs. The coney teaches us to keep our praise on. The joy of the Lord is our strength. And, the more we keep our praise on, the more territories we will gain. The coney positions himself well. How about you?

> The nugget from the coney: He positions himself well!

LESSONS FROM THE LOCUST

Interestingly, Agur extracts wisdom from the locust. What the Bible refers to as the locust will be a grasshopper to us in the West. A locust, by itself, cannot do anything great. However, when many locusts move, as a synchronized army, the devastation and feat is amazing.

Upon scrutiny, we have discovered that the locust has two "phases" of existence. Most of the time, the locust exists in solitude. Harmless and sluggish, they have a tendency to avoid other grasshoppers. However, if the locust population increases and are overcrowded, then the locust changes to the gregarious kind. The change is so remarkable that one would think it was a completely different species. The change is not in appearance or body shape but in behavior. In this gregarious phase,

Chapter 10 • Wisdom from Agur's Four Little Creatures

locusts enjoy the company of others. They unite together in swarms of billions of locusts. They cover hundreds of square miles. In the worst cases, they devour every green thing in their way. In 1889, a swarm of locusts, covering 2,000 square miles, crossed the Red Sea with an estimated weight of 500,000 tons and containing 250 billion, individual locusts. So what can we learn from the locust?

1. The locust teaches us that we can achieve more as a team than as a loner.

Many would like to succeed as the Lone Ranger and be the superstar. However, the locust teaches us the power of a team, moving toward a goal. Solomon's advice must be heeded:

> *Two are better than one; because they have a good reward for their labour. For if they fall, the one will lift up his fellow: but woe to him that is alone when he falleth; for he hath not another to help him up. Again, if two lie together, then they have heat: but how can one be warm alone? And if one prevail against him, two shall withstand him; and a threefold cord is not quickly broken.* (Ecclesiastes 4:9-12)

2. The locust teaches us that a little fire should not deter a person from his purpose.

Today, the Middle East and parts of Africa are still, occasionally, plagued by swarms of locusts. Fire is used as a deterrent to the swarm. Lit branches or heaped together car tires are meant to deter the locusts. However, the locust takes the mind set that a few might die but the fire will not deter us from our purpose. To be honest, the fires are not effective against a billion locusts. Too many of us are easily deterred by a little fire or some opposition.

3. The locust teaches us to be purpose driven and not problem minded.

The fire cannot stop them. A few casualties cannot deter them. Man, with all his wisdom and weaponry, cannot stop the locust.

Tall walls have been erected to hinder the progress of the locust. But, that does not stop the locust. He is purpose driven rather than being problem minded. The locust is opportunity minded rather than being opposition minded.

4. The locust teaches us that a unit, with a common vision, can destroy anything in its way.

The wisdom of the locust is that no matter how small you are, if you have a big vision and are united, you can destroy all opposition. Unity of vision, purpose and team make the locust undefeated.

5. The locust teaches us the power of precision.

The locust moves, as an army, toward a field. Their synchronized motion and mobilization enable them to professionally execute their objectives. They teach us the power of precision. You cannot afford to have a haphazard attitude about your dream. You must be precise. You must purposefully execute your every move. The locust does not do "hit and miss"; he is very precise.

6. The locust teaches us that everyone has a role to play.

The locust does not behave as Rambo, the Terminator or Commando, leaving the army behind and taking on the whole enemy by himself. The army of locusts teaches us that everyone is important and has an important role to play. We must learn to be team players. Do not ever underestimate your contribution to the team where God has placed you. Your input is valuable.

7. The locust teaches us to finish what you start.

When locusts are moving as an army, they will not stop for anything. They finish the job before they move on to another target. They teach us to finish what we start. Too many of us have our hands in

The nugget from the locust: He propels forward!

so many different, unfinished plates. The locust propels forward and is a finisher. Therefore, you must be a finisher.

LESSONS FROM THE SPIDER

Finally, we come to the fourth little, wise creature – the spider. To be honest, my daughter peeked my interest in the four little creatures. I travel, extensively, and spend many days away from my family because of the ministry. I always look forward to seeing my family. Jodie, my youngest child, is eight years old. She is a very bubbly and inquisitive little character. I came home from a trip to Nigeria. Before I could say anything, she ran up to me and asked, "Dad, how many eyes does the spider have?" I never gave a thought to how many eyes a spider had. Seeing the excitement in her face, I knew it could not be the conventional answer of two. She, then, showed me a picture of a spider who had eight eyes and another who had eyes all over its body. I was mesmerized by what I saw and thus began the investigations. So, what can we learn from the spider?

1. **The spider teaches us that no matter how small you are, you can go all the way to the top.**

Agur states, "The spider taketh hold with her hands, and is in kings' palaces." Notice, it winds up in the king's palace. Years ago, Zig Ziglar wrote two books titled, *See You at the Top* and *Over the Top*. To be the top is God's will for us. If the tiny little spider can be in the king's house, so can you.

2. **The spider teaches us to never rely on somebody's hands but the hands that God gave you.**

Notice the words, "The spider taketh hold with her hands..." While it is popular to look for a handout, it is not God's best for people. Relying upon the government to take care of you is not God's best.

The government can never be your El Shaddai. Only God can be your El Shaddai. Only two pair of hands can deliver you: The hands of God and your hands.

3. The spider teaches us that everything you need is already within you. It teaches us to live from the inside out.

The ant lives underground, the coney lives in a rock and the locust lives in the grass. However, the spider is the only one whose house is within himself. The ant, coney and locust have to use the exterior to build their house. Only the spider uses what he has on the inside to build his house.

The point I want to make is that your house is within you. Your car is within you. Your breakthrough is within you. Stop looking on the outside and look within you. Greater is He that is within you than he that is in the world. When Paul faced unsurmountable problems in Asia (2 Corinthians 1:8,9), he said the answer he was looking was within him. As believers, you must understand that the Holy One is within you. He has all the answers to your problems.

4. The spider teaches us to keep building when they destroy your stuff.

I am sure you have done it as many times as I have. Sometimes, I look up in the garage or outside in the garden and see a spider web. I take the broomstick and begin to dismantle the spider's web. One time, I took notice that as I was busy pulling down the spider's house, it was busy rebuilding it – even as my destruction was in process. The spider did not spend his time crying over spilled milk or over what was destroyed. As quick as his house was being dismantled, he was busy rebuilding it.

The spider teaches us that no matter what is destroyed, rebuild it again. If they dash your dream, rebuild it. If they dash your hope, rebuild it. If you built it before, then, you can do it again.

Stop crying over what you have lost – move on and rebuild. Jesus emphatically declared, "Destroy this temple and in three days I will build it again." Since all you have came from within you, even if they take it away, you can create it again.

5. The spider teaches us to walk by faith and not by sight.

What struck me when Jodie was talking to me about the spider was this: although he has many eyes, the spider cannot see properly. Therefore, he does not hunt his prey with his eyes. He does not depend upon his sight to win. Many years ago, the prophet Habakkuk said, "The just shall live by faith." (Habakkuk 2:4) Paul revealed, "We walk by faith and not by sight." (2 Corinthians 5:7)

6. The spider teaches us that we need the oil of the Holy Spirit so we won't get stuck.

The spider's web is sticky. His prey gets entangled and becomes food for the spider. What is amazing is how the spider can glide across the *same* sticky web that made another creature a prey. This is due to the oil that is secreted from the follicles of the spider's feet. The oil causes him to glide without getting stuck.

The oil is symbolic of the anointing of the Holy Spirit. We all need the anointing upon our lives. What causes others to be stuck and become prey does not need to be your reality as you operate under the anointing of the Spirit. Every believer and business man must walk in the anointing. It is the anointing that makes the difference.

7. The spider teaches us to always be productive.

The spider's philosophy is that in order to succeed in life, one must be a producer. Take what you have from the inside… outside. As you are reading the closing words of this book, know this: There is a great deposit of wealth and blessing inside of you. Paul told us that "we have treasure in earthen vessels." (2 Corinthians 4)

When you change from being a consumer to being a producer, you will fulfill the very first command that God gave the Adamic race, "Be fruitful, multiply, subdue and dominate the earth." (Genesis 1:28)

The spider demands that you are productive. The only way you can dominate the earth is by being a producer. Look at Steve Jobs and Bill Gates. These two men have dominated the world with their products. I want you to know that there is something within *you* to dominate the world. There's something in *you* that will give you the influence God desires for you to have. Are you ready to be like the spider and be a producer?

> The nugget from the spider: He produces!

In conclusion – The ant prepares; The coney positions; The locust propels; The spider produces. You need to prepare to position yourself to propel forward by being a producer.

Go take your world by storm. The world is waiting for you!

ABOUT THE AUTHOR

Dr. Glenn Arekion is a uniquely gifted teacher and conference speaker. He conveys the Word of Truth in a simple, yet dynamic and motivational way. With over two decades of experience, he travels the globe mentoring leaders, equipping businessmen and ministering to people, helping them to fulfill their purpose in life. He is a captivating and much sought after speaker.

Glenn is dedicated to transforming lives from defeat into victory. His teaching materials are sold in many countries and are very popular among those with a desire to grow strong in faith and experience great success. He is also the author of 28 books.

Glenn is apostolic in his thrust of ministry. He believes in establishing churches, teaching and training pastors in their calling. His television program, Faithlift, airs twice a week on The Word Network. Faithlift is also a daily television program on the Faithworld Channel in the U.K. and all over Europe.

Born in Mauritius, Africa, but raised and educated in London, Glenn holds Master's degrees from Life Christian University in Florida and International College of Excellence in Chicago. He also holds a doctorate degree in theology from the prestigious Destiny College in Florida.

Glenn and his beautiful wife, Rosanna, have three children: Lisa, Ethan and Jodie and reside in Kentucky.

AUTHOR CONTACT

Glenn Arekeon Ministries
P. O. Box 197777
Louisville, KY 40259
mail@glennarekion.org
glennarekion.org

www.ingramcontent.com/pod-product-compliance
Lightning Source LLC
LaVergne TN
LVHW051506070426
835507LV00022B/2953